F O R

COMPUTER
BUFFS

& Other
Technological Types

CAREERS

FOR

COMPUTER BUFFS

& Other Technological Types

Marjorie Eberts
Margaret Gisler

VGM Career Horizons
a division of *NTC Publishing Group*
Lincolnwood, Illinois USA

ABF 4493

MAR 1 8 1997

Library of Congress Cataloging-in-Publication Data

Eberts, Marjorie.
    Careers for computer buffs & other technological types /
Marjorie Eberts, Margaret Gisler.
        p.   cm.
    ISBN 0-8442-4104-0 (hard).—ISBN 0-8442-4105-9 (soft)
    1. Computers—Vocational guidance.   2. Electronic data processing—
Vocational guidance.   I. Gisler, Margaret.   II. Title.
    QA76.25.E23   1993
004′.023′73—dc20   93-10584
                                                                        CIP

1996 Printing

Published by VGM Career Horizons, a division of NTC Publishing Group.
© 1994 by NTC Publishing Group, 4255 West Touhy Avenue,
Lincolnwood (Chicago), Illinois 60646-1975 U.S.A.
All rights reserved. No part of this book may be reproduced, stored
in a retrieval system, or transmitted in any form or by any means,
electronic, mechanical, photocopying, recording or otherwise, without
the prior permission of NTC Publishing Group.
Manufactured in the United States of America.

    6 7 8 9 0 VP 9 8 7 6 5 4 3

Dedication

To our computer buff husbands, Marvin and Les, from whom we have learned so much about computers.

Contents

About the Authors

Marjorie Eberts and Margaret Gisler have been writing professionally for fourteen years. They are prolific free-lance authors with more than sixty books in print. Their writing is usually in the field of education. The two authors have written textbooks, beginning readers, and study-skills books for schoolchildren. They also have written a book on preparing children for kindergarten and a college preparation handbook. This is their fifth book on careers.

Beside writing books, the two authors have a syndicated education column, "Dear Teacher," which appears in newspapers throughout the country. Eberts and Gisler also give advice on educational issues in speeches, at workshops, and on television.

Writing this book was a special pleasure for the authors, as it gave them the opportunity to talk to so many fellow computer buffs. The book was created on computers located in two different states, and chapters were exchanged by modem for further editing.

Eberts is a graduate of Stanford University, and Gisler is a graduate of Ball State and Butler universities. Both received their specialist degrees in education from Butler University.

Acknowledgments

We would especially like to thank the following computer buffs who introduced us to so many of the computer buffs about whom we wrote in this book.

Bob Gorshe
Matt Kelsey
Karl Schwartz
Lani Sutherland

Jobs for Computer Buffs

Do people often find you exercising your mouse instead of your dog? Do you grab your laptop instead of a book when you go on vacation? Are you more likely to find out the current temperature in Minneapolis or Los Angeles by using an on-line information service instead of glancing through the local newspaper? Is your favorite chair at home in front of a computer or a television set? Would you prefer to win a game of chess with a computer instead of a local expert? Have you ever crashed a plane trying to land on the runway on your computer screen? If you answered a resounding "yes" to most of these questions, you are definitely a computer buff.

Everyone today needs to be computer literate to some extent to survive. Computer buffs, however, are a special breed. They try to spend as much of their waking time as they can working or playing on their computers. The magnetic pull of the computer dictates almost everything they do. They balance their checkbooks and study the stock market on the computer. Most have forsaken pen and paper correspondence for e-mail. Computer buffs spend hours browsing through computer stores or studying computer magazines to make sure that they know about the latest hardware and software. Contemplating how they can increase their computer's memory is another favored pastime, as is devising new programs to meet their needs. The computer invades virtually every aspect of a computer buff's everyday life. You will even find confirmed computer buffs playing solitaire on computers.

Even though they have logged thousands of hours in front of their terminals, computer buffs never lose their passion for working or playing on their machines. The more time they spend on their computers, the more they are drawn to explore the myriad activities that computers make possible, from creating art to educating themselves on almost every subject.

Computer buffs do not have to limit their interest in computers to the role of a hobby. They can readily find satisfying careers that will let them spend their working hours in jobs devoted entirely to the computer. The computer revolution is here, and new and exciting jobs in the industry are emerging at an astonishing speed. Just thirty years ago only large companies had computers. Today there is scarcely a business or industry that does not utilize the computer in some way. From agriculture to aerospace, there are exciting careers for computer buffs. The computer was *Time* magazine's Man of the Year in 1982. Working with a computer will be the job of the twenty-first century.

The Birth and Growth of the Computer

The computer's parents were the mathematicians and scientists who desired a machine that would reduce the time required to do complex mathematical calculations. Their first efforts resulted in the invention of the abacus approximately five thousand years ago. The ancient Babylonians, Egyptians, Chinese, Greeks, and Romans all used devices with movable counters to improve the speed and accuracy of their calculations. It was not until the 1600s, however, that the first mechanical calculating machines were built. One of the more notable machines was built in 1642 by Blaise Pascal, a French mathematician and scientist, to help handle his father's business accounts. Pascal's machine used rotating wheels with teeth to add and subtract numbers of up to eight digits. The name "Pascal" is remembered today by computer buffs every time they use the computer language that bears his name. Just a few years later, in 1673, Gottfried Leibniz developed a more complex calculating device that also had the capability of multiplying, dividing, and finding square roots. Early calculating machines were not reliable, and all had problems carrying over numbers in addition. Mathematicians, scientists, engineers, navigators, and others who needed to do more than very simple calculations were forced to rely on printed mathematical tables that were riddled with errors. Disconcerted by the enormous effort required to make calculation tables, Charles Babbage, an English mathematician, developed the idea of an automatic calculating device called the "difference engine." Financial and technical difficulties precluded the building of the complete machine; however, the section of the machine that was completed is regarded as the first automatic calculator. Nevertheless, Babbage is not primarily remembered for the difference engine but for his design of a machine that he called the "analytical engine." This machine, which was designed to perform complicated calculations, contained the basic elements of modern electronic computers. Babbage's machine separated memory and storage and was programmable. Babbage kept developing and refining the design of this machine until his death; however, the problems that had beset him in attempting to build the difference engine discouraged him from making a concerted effort to build the analytical engine.

Interest waned in the development of automatic calculation machines after Babbage's death. Progress was made, however, in developing calculators. By the end of the 1800s, reliable calculating machines were readily available. In addition, data processing became automated through Herman Hollerith's development of an automatic punch-card tabulating machine. He had been commissioned by the United States Census Bureau to resolve the crisis the bureau faced in handling the 1890 census data. Millions of immigrants had turned the process of analyzing the 1880 census data into an almost eight-year task. With the nation growing so rapidly, the Census Bureau feared that the 1890 census data would never be analyzed before the next census was taken. Herman Hollerith's data processing device saved the day permitting the 1890 census data to be analyzed in just two and one-half years. Hollerith had developed a code that used a pattern of punched holes to represent data. His machine recognized whether or not a hole was covered, and electricity passed through the holes activating motors that moved counters which gave out totals. Number-crunching industries such as accounting, banking, and insurance enthusiastically embraced the use of perforated cards to handle data. In fact, punched card equipment was used in data processing until the late 1950s. Even today some elements of Hollerith's code still are being used in computers to read input and format output. The Tabulating Machine Company that Hollerith organized to sell equipment for commercial use went on to become one of the companies that merged together to form IBM in 1911.

The First-Generation Computers

After Hollerith constructed his tabulating machine, several computing devices were developed. These computers were never well publicized. ENIAC (Electronic Numerical Integrator Analyzer and Computer), however, gained instant worldwide attention when it was introduced at a press conference in 1946. ENIAC was a gigantic machine—over one hundred feet long and eight feet deep and weighing eighty tons—developed by J. Presper Eckert and John W. Mauchly, two engineers at the University of Pennsylvania. ENIAC, the first fully electronic digital computer, worked approximately one thousand times faster than previous machines. It could perform five thousand arithmetic operations in a second. ENIAC proved that large electronic systems were technically possible. Unfortunately, ENIAC had a serious flaw as it was very time consuming to program because switches had to be set and boards had to be wired by hand. It would take days to set up programs that would take only seconds to run. In spite of its flaws, ENIAC inaugurated the modern computer age.

John von Neumann solved ENIAC's flaws by introducing the idea that programs could be coded as numbers and stored with data in a computer's memory. His idea was used in building EDVAC (Electronic Discrete Variable Automatic Computer), which was the first stored-program digital computer.

By 1945, the Census Bureau was again drowning in a sea of paper. Eckert and Mauchly signed a contract to develop a new computer to solve the bureau's problems. They also contracted to build computers for three other clients: Northrop Aircraft Corporation, Prudential Life Insurance, and the A. C. Nielsen Company. Eckert and Mauchly developed a more advanced electronic digital computer for their customers, which they called UNIVAC I (UNIVersal Automatic Computer). Unfortunately, their financial skills did not match their computer expertise, and they were forced to sell the company to Remington Rand in 1950. UNIVAC achieved fame in 1952 when it was introduced to television to predict the results of the presidential election. UNIVAC predicted that Eisenhower would win in a landslide, but the people at CBS did not agree with the prediction. The next day everyone learned that the computer had been correct and the humans incorrect. Remington Rand's success with UNIVAC inspired Thomas Watson, Jr., to have IBM enter the fledgling computer business. Within a few years, IBM secured a dominant position in the industry with its moderately priced computers, which tied easily into existing punch-card installations.

The Second-Generation Computers

ENIAC and UNIVAC I used vacuum tubes for arithmetic and memory-switching functions. These tubes were very expensive, used considerable power, and gave off an enormous amount of heat. In 1948, the transistor was invented at Bell Telephone Laboratories, spelling the end of the vacuum tube. Other solid-state devices were invented in the 1950s and 1960s. By using this new technology, second-generation computers became much smaller than earlier computers, had increased storage capacity, and were able to process data much faster.

The Third-Generation Computers

The invention of the integrated circuit in 1958 by Jack Kilby of Texas Instruments signaled the start of the third generation of computers. Previously, individual components had to be wired together; now it was possible to print the wiring and the components together on silicon circuit chips. As the transistors of the second generation of computers were replaced with integrated circuits, computers became even smaller, faster, and less expensive. Furthermore, integrated circuits permitted the design of computers with tremendous memory capacity. The need for reliable software packages for third-generation computers generated the birth of the software industry. In addition, the advances in solid-state technology of this generation of computers led to the development of the minicomputer.

The Fourth-Generation Computers and Beyond

Today's computers are fourth-generation machines with increased computing speed using even tinier and more densely packed circuits. In addition, this further miniaturization of integrated circuits—VLSI (Very Large Scale Integration)—has led to the emergence of microcomputers and the phenomenal growth in home computer sales. With each generation of computers the computing speed has increased, the size of computers has decreased, and the price has gone down. It is simply amazing to realize how rapidly the computer has developed. All of the impressive power of the mighty ENIAC built in 1946 can be contained today on a single microchip. The fifth generation of computers is now on the horizon, promising computers with ever more capabilities as they (computers) learn how to learn (imitate human learning).

A Computer Buff's Dream— A Career with the Machine

The inventors of the first computers had no idea of the numerous ways computers would be used. Today computer buffs can find jobs in almost every workplace. Just a glance at the following newspaper ads shows the diversity of jobs that exist for computer buffs:

Software Technical Support Specialist   The inside software technical support specialist resolves software support inquiries and provides assistance to customers via phone, fax, or modem. The position also tests software and communicates with software engineers to develop/document end-user software manuals.

Qualifications include: one year technical support/customer service experience with a microcomputer software/hardware company, excellent oral/written communication and organizational skills, computer literacy, AA degree in computer science, business, or related field preferred. Must be able to maintain positive customer contact, prioritize multiple projects, and meet deadlines. (Computer Publishing Firm)

Programmer/Analyst   We have a position available for programmer/analyst for our PC-based Paradox data base. Position requires one to two years of relational data base technical support in a Novell LAN environment, preferably using PAL code. Qualified applicant must be a team player with excellent analytical and communication skills and MS-DOS and PC configuration experience. (Federal Credit Union)

SYSTEMS ENGINEER   A National LAN/WAN network integration company seeks systems engineer for new branch. Position requires extensive knowledge of operating systems (Novell and/ or LAN Manager), proficiency in installation, configuration, and troubleshooting of LAN-based applications software, (Windows, gateways, word processing, document management). Strong customer service orientation and troubleshooting ability a must as well as two-plus years proven field experience. CNE a plus. (National LAN/WAN Network Integration Company)

MAC SYSTEMS ADMINISTRATOR   Develop an automated systems approach to maintain and support a thirty-user system that could double in size in the next five years. Document, quantify, and standardize computer systems for users. Must have strong knowledge of MAC networking and preferably know 4D software. (Computer Employment Agency)

COMPUTER DESIGNER   Growing innovative design firm seeking individual with the following skills: minimum two years experience with Macintosh software (Quark, Photoshop, Illustrator, Freehand); strong knowledge of type, design principles, basic copywriting, and 4/C process printing. Basic principles of marketing a plus. (Advertising Design Firm)

NETWORK MANAGER—RADIOLOGY   Design, install, and manage a PC-based computer network to link together faculty and staff within the university radiology departments. The network will be used for communication, word processing, data base management, image processing, patient information, and education. B.S. degree in computer science, computer engineering, or a related area required, as is a minimum of five years experience in computer network administration, PC support, computing, and data base management. (University Medical Center)

DATA ENTRY   Business credit reporting service needs employee to perform input of credit information into data base. Good spelling skills, must type 45wpm on test. Full-time, 8:00–4:45. (Credit Reporting Service)

COMPUTER PROGRAMMER   North side commercial printing company is seeking C or C++ programmer with 3–7 years experience. Novell networking, internetworking skills, FORTRAN, and data format conversion are desired but not required. PC-DOS and Sun Unix platform. (Printing Company)

CAD INSTRUCTOR   For CAD drafting program. A minimum of bachelor's degree or equivalent in drafting or related technical field and at least three years field experience. Experience in education or vocational/technical education is preferred. Must have strong math skills, applied physics background, and a good knowledge of AutoCad release 10. Hours 1:00 P.M.–10:00 P.M., five days. (Technical Institute)

WORD PROCESSOR   MacIntosh and IBM MS Word 5.0 and 5.5, Windows, WordPerfect, Paradox, Lotus, and Excel skills are needed. (Temporary Jobs Agency)

COMPUTER SOFTWARE   West side reseller is looking for a seasoned rep for our software. Experience must include: micros, job cost accounting software, construction cost codes, and sales skills. (Software Reseller)

This book is dedicated to helping all computer buffs realize their dreams of finding jobs that will allow them to work with computers on company time. Here is a bird's-eye view of some of the jobs that you will read about in this book.

Creating the Computer

People with vision are employed to create mainframes, minicomputers, and microcomputers as well as the peripheral devices essential to their operation. Jobs are not limited to research and development, as computers need to be manufactured, sold, and serviced. What's more, no machine can be sold without the manufacturer both documenting how the machine is to be used and training the user to operate it, if necessary. Some computers are so complex that customers require continuing technical and support service.

Developing the Software

Developing software is very labor intensive. Programmers are needed to write the system software every computer requires to manage its operation. Programmers also are needed to create the programs that tell the computer how to perform specific tasks. Besides developing software programs, computer buffs are needed to sell the programs and provide documentation and training for program users.

Providing Computer Services

As the number of computers in the United States approaches 100 million units, more and more people are needed to provide a variety of services to computer users. A growing employment area exists for those who can plan, design, and implement computer systems and networks. Furthermore, with so many companies drowning in paperwork, transaction processing services need employees to process all kinds of transactions from payroll to medical records. The current explosion of information also has led to the creation of information service providers who use computers to collect, manipulate, and disseminate information about all kinds of topics from stock market quotations to statistics on school enrollment.

Solving Users' Problems

Systems analysts do not just burrow their noses in computers. They are professional problem solvers who listen to computer users in order to meet their needs and solve their problems. Systems analysts improve existing systems and may even design new systems. All of their work is designed to give users the computer resources they need. Systems analysts are the "people-persons" in the computer profession.

Running Computer Systems

Computer systems must be kept running. For many companies that means round-the-clock jobs for computer systems operators. The computers and all their related machines must operate smoothly. When the systems are down, the operations staff must get them on-line again as quickly as possible. Running the computer also involves entering data and instructions into the computer and handling the computer's output. Furthermore, librarians are needed in some organizations to catalog, file, and check out magnetic tapes and disks.

Managing Information Systems

Computers no longer are used just to handle everyday business tasks such as billing and payroll. Now computers are providing all types of information that help management make decisions about products, sales, marketing, and almost every aspect of a company's business. Computers have the capacity to spew out so much information that managers are now required to manage the data bases of stored corporate information material and direct what new material should be developed. Besides handling these new tasks, managers of information systems purchase equipment and software and supervise all the other data-processing tasks.

Using the Computer in Special Areas—Design, Manufacturing, Animation, Music, and Entertainment

Computer buffs can use the computer to express their creativity whether it is in design, manufacturing, animation, music, or entertainment. One of the fastest growing areas of computer use is CAD (computer-aided design). Here there are jobs that let computer buffs design and plan automobiles, houses, clothing, and such computer staples as microchips and integrated circuits on the computer. CAM (computer-aided manufacturing) lets people be involved with the fabrication of products under computer control. If you have an artistic flair, you can find jobs that combine this talent with your interest in the computer. For example, in the music arena you can use the computer to create compositions and play a variety of instruments. You also can use the amazing graphics capacity of computers to create commercial artwork and all types of entertainment from books, to TV shows, and movies.

Using the Computer on the Job

Banks, insurance companies, retailers, hospitals, and manufacturers all have computers actively playing a role in the operation of their businesses. Airlines, supermarkets, and newspapers use computers to conduct their daily business. No matter what occupation you choose from A to Z, whether it is an airline pilot, a doctor, a librarian, or a zookeeper, you will find yourself using the computer in your job.

Exploring Future Computer Careers

The range of job options for computer buffs will continue to widen throughout the 1990s and into the twenty-first century.

Completely new jobs will emerge as computers become more skilled at making decisions, learn to read handwriting better, understand the human voice, communicate better with other computers, and just become "smarter." Even more new careers will appear as wireless communication increases and Hollywood and the computer become more closely linked. At the same time, emerging technology will change the nature of many jobs, and some of today's jobs will disappear.

Job Qualifications

Computer buffs seem to be welded to their machines. The unbreakable bonds they forge with their computers may lead them to gain such expertise that no special training will be required for them to begin their careers in the computer industry. Computer buffs with the appropriate know-how may be employed with little training in such jobs as computer service technicians, salespeople, telecommunications technicians, desktop publishers, and computer operators. Today more and more applicants for professional-level jobs in the computer industry have college degrees. Some computer buffs (Bill Gates of Microsoft Corporation and Steven Jobs of Apple Computer and NeXT Computer, Inc.) have been extremely successful without completing college. Nevertheless, as the computer industry matures, more and more firms are requiring successful applicants for professional-level positions to have college degrees. Although majors in computer science did not exist thirty years ago, companies are increasingly expecting those who are interested in the technical or systems side of computers to have this degree from a quality program. In appendix A, you will find a list of accredited programs in computer engineering and science. Since computers are used in so many different arenas, job applicants have an advantage if they combine computer study with another area such as engineering, mathematics, logic, economics, business, science, art, or music.

As is true in most occupations today, successful applicants for computer positions will have logged many hours in part-time jobs, in internships, or in cooperative education programs in the computer field before applying for full-time positions.

Where the Jobs Are

Have you ever heard the song "Do You Know the Way to San Jose?" If you are interested in the creation or development of hardware or software, you better start humming this tune. For many computer buffs, relocation to San Jose or Silicon Valley in California will be essential to finding employment. California has 43.5 percent of the computer companies in the United States, and San Jose is home for more than 9 percent of those companies. The next four states having a considerable number of computer companies are Massachusetts, Illinois, New York, and Texas. The following graph will show computer buffs where computer companies are located:

Computer Company Locations

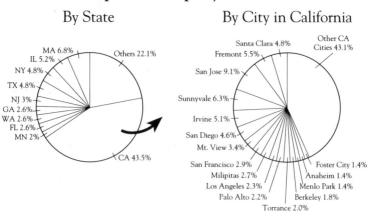

By State   By City in California

Published with permission from Computer Industry Almanac. Copyright © 1992,Computer Industry Almanac, Inc., 225 Allen Way, Incline Village, Nevada 89451–9608.

Computer jobs are certainly not limited to computer companies. An increasing number of jobs exist with firms providing computer services, and an ever-growing demand for employees with computer expertise exists for almost every employer from Fortune 500 companies to very small firms to all branches of the government. The future is bright for computer buffs wherever they may choose to work. According to the American Electronics Association, one of every twenty jobs in the United States is in electronics or an industry that would not exist without electronics.

Learning Even More about Computer Careers

Computer buffs know that the computer industry is changing so rapidly that books can be outdated even before they make it to the library shelf. Being aware of what is going on in the computer industry is absolutely essential for finding the perfect job. Reading periodicals and professional journals is one of the best ways to keep abreast of what is happening in the world of computers. Computer buffs interested in the latest statistics on all aspects of computing should look at a copy of the *Computer Industry Almanac*, which is available in libraries or by contacting Computer Industry Almanac, Inc., 225 Allen Way, Incline Village, Nevada 89451–8610 (tel. 702–831–8610). Published annually this almanac will give you information on salaries, employment trends, education, computer organizations and users groups, and almost everything you could possibly want to know about the computer industry.

You also can learn more about computer careers and the computer industry by contacting the many professional organizations associated with the industry. You will find a list of some of these organizations in appendix B.

CHAPTER TWO

Creating the Computer

A computer is made up of a microchip or a network of microchips and circuitry. A computer system is composed of the computer itself plus peripheral equipment, which includes such things as keyboards, mice, joysticks, monitors, printers, disks, and tapes. Everything that is part of a computer system is called hardware, while all the programs that make the computer work are called software. Those who are actively involved in the design and development of hardware are usually called hardware engineers. Of course, assemblers, inspectors, technicians, production staff, product managers, quality control experts, sales and marketing people, education specialists, technical writers, and maintenance people also play a key role in bringing computers to individuals and organizations.

If you want to be part of creating a computer, you will typically work at a computer or computer component vendor from Apple to IBM to Motorola to thousands of other companies. You may be involved in the creation of an entire computer system, just the computer, parts used in computers, or peripherals. No longer are jobs concentrated at mainframe manufacturers; now it is highly possible that you will work at a company that manufactures chips, disk drives, or other components that can be used with different computers. You may find a job within a large, well-established company such as Hewlett-Packard Co., Digital

Equipment Corporation (DEC), and Control Data Corporation (CDC) or at a newly established company. But you are more likely to work in California than anywhere else as 43.5 percent of the computer companies are located there.

If you are seriously thinking about a career in the computer industry, you must keep track of current trends to make solid career decisions. For example, in the early 1980s there were three distinct classes of computers: mainframes, minicomputers, and microcomputers. Now this distinction has blurred. A cutting edge microcomputer may be more powerful than a mainframe of just ten years' vintage, and some powerful microcomputers that are equipped with remote terminals have been changed into minicomputers. Furthermore, competition is so fierce in the computer industry that giant firms can stumble, and newcomers can rapidly disappear.

Hardware Engineering

Whenever you see a finished computer product, whether it is a minicomputer or a printer, an engineer had to play a big role in its creation. These engineers must have considerable technical prowess to design, develop, test, and maintain computers and peripheral equipment. Many will hold advanced degrees in complementary fields. Thus an engineer with a bachelor's degree in electrical engineering also might have a master's degree in computer engineering. At the same time, engineers wanting to hold managerial positions may get advanced degrees in business.

As far as advancement goes, engineers enjoying hands-on experience can choose to stay on the technical side climbing the career path to such positions as senior or principal engineer. Others can elect to become managers or supervisors, roles in which most of their time is devoted to managerial responsibilities, and only a limited time is spent on engineering.

Developing a Microprocessor

A microprocessor is an integrated circuit on a silicon chip. Equip it with primary and secondary storage and input and output devices and you have a microcomputer. Much of the engineering work in hardware occurs at the chip level. Just out of college with a degree in electrical engineering, Curtis Shrote wanted to design chips. Those positions, however, were filled on the microprocessor team he joined at Motorola. Nevertheless, Curtis chose this job because he liked the idea of being on a team assigned to develop a general purpose microprocessor that had 1.3 million devices on it and would run the software for an operating system. The microprocessor was being designed for the workstation market and would go into a computer the size of a pizza box.

When Curtis first came to Motorola, the design team had already talked to customers and decided what they wanted on the chip. The original team ranged from fifty to one hundred members, mostly electrical engineers. The project was headed by three first-line managers who dealt with the team members on a daily basis. One was a senior design engineer whose job was to see that everything was done correctly and to oversee the junior engineers and less experienced engineers like Curtis. There were also subteams, and Curtis was assigned to the cache team. (A *cache* is a storage area that keeps frequently accessed data or program instructions readily available.) His subteam of five core people, which consisted of three engineers with master's degrees, one with a bachelor's degree and prior design experience, and Curtis, clearly illustrated the level of expertise hardware engineers must have.

This subteam was responsible for logic design, data cache control, and instruction cache control. Curtis was given the responsibility of debugging (locating and correcting errors on) the cache control unit on the chip. This involved designing an external simulation environment and writing test cases for all cache areas on the chip. Once the chip was in real silicon, he checked what could not be simulated earlier.

Projects at Motorola typically take from six months to four years to complete. Curtis's project has taken four years and is currently winding down. His subteam has been downsized, and Curtis is starting to do some design work as he corrects errors. Curtis also has started working on a new project. Now that he is more experienced, he will be working on designing a next-generation microprocessor. Curtis has begun to advance along the career path toward being a senior engineer, a position that requires considerable work experience. Right now he doesn't know if he will opt in the long run to follow a technical or managerial path. He has, however, begun working on his master's degree in computer engineering, a move that Motorola strongly supports. He is getting his degree from National Technological University by taking ABET (Accreditation Board for Engineering and Technology) courses on site and on company time. The courses are live or pretaped presentations of courses approved by ABET that have been taught and recorded at their actual schools. Curtis can even phone and talk to the instructors of these courses. It is quite important for individuals wishing to have a solid background in hardware engineering to be graduates of a school with an accredited computer science or engineering program. A list of these schools can be found in appendix A.

As a child Curtis was thoroughly intrigued by the computers at his father's workplace. Furthermore, his father, an information systems manager, would talk to his family all the time about the business side of computers. By junior high, Curtis had decided that he wanted a career in the computer industry. After investigating a number of schools, Curtis elected to go to Purdue University and obtain a dual degree accredited in both electrical and computer engineering. Although initially he was not interested in taking part in the school's co-op program, interviews with companies participating in the program made him change his mind. Cooperative education programs let students alternate studying at college with an off-campus job. Students are able to earn all or a great part of the cost of college. The Purdue program required five semesters of work to obtain a cooperative education certificate. Curtis actually worked off-campus in the computer industry for six semesters.

Students must interview with companies and be selected by them in order to participate in the co-op program. Curtis had several choices, and he decided on a co-op program at the IBM facility in Kingston, New York. There he was assigned to work in facilities engineering updating building floor plans. Although Curtis had his heart set on being in chip design, he knew it was not realistic to get such a position for a first assignment. Nevertheless, he was quite pleased to be working for a major computer firm as co-op experiences often lead to job offers in the future. Like all co-op students, Curtis had to interview for each subsequent off-campus job. Since IBM lets you change departments, he moved to the innerconnect products group after his first co-op experience and stayed with this department working on a variety of projects for the rest of his time off-campus. The department built network boxes that interconnect mainframes and mainframes with peripherals. Although he wasn't able to do design work, he had the advantage of working with an actual design, saw a long-term project evolve from simulation to actual system integration, and observed the turnover in management and employees. Curtis believes that working at IBM in the cooperative education program gave him a better idea of the courses he needed at school plus the obvious benefit of experience in the computer industry. In the semester before graduation, Curtis interviewed with five companies and was offered a job by every one.

Working in Research and Development

A job in research and development is the dream of many computer buffs who are eager to be involved in the front end of developing a product. For Loyal Mealer, this dream became a reality when he started his career in the computer industry as an engineer (entry-level position) in research and development in the Scientific Instruments Division at Hewlett-Packard Co. He was able to dive immediately into working on the design of an analog/digital board for a research-grade mass spectrometer—work that was done almost entirely on a computer. Loyal was able to design immediately because of his hobby and work experience and because many schools are now giving their students experience in designing. He holds a bachelor's degree in electrical engineering/computer science. Without design experience at college, he would have needed a master's degree to handle this job.

After one year, Loyal became a hardware design engineer. For the next few years, he designed many circuit boards and was even the sole designer for one product (all boards), which was fun and immensely satisfying work. Loyal became a hardware technical lead and then a project manager doing the hardware design for an array processor board. Now, just twelve years after starting with Hewlett-Packard, he is a section manager for electronics and research-grade mass spectrometers in the research and development department. In this position, he manages ten engineers and two project managers. This involves evaluating their work and managing their career paths. He also manages some projects directly. Although he sometimes will offer engineers design help, Loyal says that the higher you climb in management, the harder it is to return to the technical side. For individuals in his position, the next career step is into a research and development lab manager position or some type of marketing or manufacturing management position. Loyal points out that as growth has slowed in the computer industry so have the possibilities for advancement. Furthermore, it is now more difficult for college graduates to find entry-level positions in design. Loyal advises graduates with this goal to start in manufacturing so they can learn how to solve design problems as a stepping-stone to a job in research and development.

Director of Applications Engineering for a Microchip Company

The design of any complex machine or system—be it an automobile or a microchip—is always broken down into several specialized areas. For an automobile, you will find designers in charge of designing engines, transmissions, radiators, and safety door locks. For a microchip, there are physicists who know how to implant the right kind of impurity to make the silicon the right kind of semiconductor and to interconnect circuits with the right kind of metal. There are also circuit designers who know how to pack transistors as tightly as possible, and there are logic designers who can implement any desired logic function at the highest speed using the smallest possible number of transistors.

Designers start with a requirement to develop a specific microchip. They bring to their individual areas of design a perspective on such things as producibility, reliability, functionality, power consumption, ways to achieve the highest operating speed, and lowest cost. On the other side are the purchasers (users) of microchips who are concerned with the whole chip—how it will fit into their systems and what portion of a given task the microchip will do. These are the people who are using microchips in medical equipment, computers, printers, cellular telephones, gas pumps, and so forth.

At Xilinx, a maker of microchips, the views of the designers and users are brought together so that the company makes a chip that users want. Peter Alfke, director of applications engineering, tells the designers what the users want and communicates to the users what Xilinx chips can do. This is not a simple task, as it requires good communication skills plus a solid technical background. Peter meets these requirements handily as he holds a master's degree in electrical engineering, has worked as a design engineer and design team manager for ten years, and has been in applications engineering for twenty-five years working alone or with up to one hundred people reporting to him. Besides finding out what users want in new chips, Peter consults with users on any problems they are having using the company's existing microchips. His job is not a traditional engineering job as he spends so much of his time writing and talking about his company's products and users. Nevertheless, without his engineering background, he would not be able to bring the different perspectives of designers and users together, and his company would not be making the chips Xilinx customers want.

Providing Technical Help and Support to Computer Users

Computer users have always needed help when problems occur. Their problems are frequently solved by customer service calls or actual visits from technical support specialists. For computer buffs who are intrigued by the challenge of analyzing and solving users' problems, jobs as customer and technical support specialists can be quite satisfying. You usually need to have a strong background in computer science coupled with an ability to devise creative solutions to diverse problems in order to handle these jobs. Support specialists will typically work for computer and computer component manufacturers or large user organizations. Your career path may lead to positions in management, or you may elect to remain a troubleshooter.

A Technical Support Representative

Ashley Dunham works for Hayes Microcomputer Products, Inc., as a technical support representative. She spends her workdays answering users' questions about the company's data communications products as well as general communications questions. Most of her time is spent on the phone helping users with problems, but she also answers letters from customers as well as e-mail queries. Although Ashley had a computer science degree as well as several years experience working in the college computer science center as a user assistant, she still needed on-the-job training at Hayes to learn about users' problems and how to help them work through these problems.

Ashley became so fascinated with computers in high school that her father actually gave her a computer. She also had the opportunity to spend half of her school day at a science center where she had classes two hours each day in computer science. In college, she specialized in programming and data communications, and her goal now is to incorporate the two in her work. Ashley is very pleased with her current job as a technical support representative as she genuinely enjoys helping people and working in the computer industry. Demand for support specialists is strong and should continue to grow.

Selling and Servicing Computers in Retail Stores

According to the *Computer Industry Almanac*, 25 percent of the households in the United States have a computer at home. Furthermore, in many organizations employees have desktop PCs for office use and laptop or notebook computers for use on the road. And the number of computers is expected to continue to grow in the next ten years. The amazing growth in PCs has resulted in an equally amazing growth in the number of stores selling PCs. But this is not all these stores sell; they also sell peripheral devices from printers to mice. You also will find them selling an astounding number of accessories to help computers run smoother and supplies such as paper, ribbons, and printer cartridges. Many stores also rent, lease, and repair computers. Some offer training and consultations. Computer buffs can find a variety of jobs in computer stores, department stores, discount stores, and mail-order and catalog firms. The opportunities for employment are good in this area, as there are more than 25,000 stores and businesses selling computer products in the United States, according to the *Computer Industry Almanac*.

Owning and Operating a Computer Store

Twelve years ago, Alfonso Li went to a computer show and saw a booth that was labeled "franchising." Shortly thereafter, he was the owner of a MicroAge computer store. After some initial training, he opened his store and worked in both sales and repair with only two employees to help him. Today, he owns and manages a larger store, is doing some sales work, and has twenty-five employees. This business takes a lot of his time—it is decidedly not a nine-to-five job.

Every day since Alfonso opened his MicroAge store, he has spent time learning more about computers. He reads, goes to seminars and schools, and talks to manufacturers. Technology is advancing so rapidly that Alfonso says everything would be changed if he took a six-month vacation and then returned to the computer business.

Alfonso has been able to respond well to the changes in the computer retail business because of his strong business background. Besides having an M.B.A., he also worked as a corporate controller for seven years. The focus of his store has changed since computers have become so much cheaper and computer users so much more knowledgeable. With profits disappearing from the sale of PCs, Alfonso has shifted more into selling high-end and expensive computers. He also has greatly expanded services to customers in setting up and getting their computers running, including programming. His store also sells software and peripherals. Because he could not find good technicians, Alfonso set up a school for technicians at his store two years ago. Successful store owners cannot just be computer buffs; they also must have a solid understanding of business and be prepared to work long hours.

Working in a Computer Store

Behind every computer sold in a computer store there is usually a salesperson. The more computers salespeople sell, the more they are likely to earn from commissions. Although no formal course of study is required for these positions, salespeople need to be knowledgeable about the computers and equipment they sell. They also need to be willing to work long hours. Store owners like Alfonso Li are looking for skilled technicians who have completed a community college or training school program in repair work.

Employment Trends

The computer industry is maturing. While growth is no longer as explosive, this industry is still expanding. Where jobs for hardware professionals were once concentrated at mainframe manufacturers, they now are distributed among companies that make computer components. Demand should remain high for professionals in networking and communications as technology is changing so rapidly in these areas. And because products are becoming so complicated, an increased need for sales and marketing professionals with computer expertise exists.

Developing the Software

Y ou are using software when you write a report, create graphics for presentations, or make a spreadsheet on a computer. Visit any store selling software, and you will see the vast amount of software that has been created for business, pleasure, and education. Many individuals are involved in developing software and delivering it to retail stores, businesses, and other organizations. There are careers in software for developers, salespeople, marketing experts, advertisers, teachers, trainers, writers, managers, and researchers to name just a few areas. Nevertheless, the central figure in the development of software is the programmer.

Computers can do only what they have been told to do, and the people who tell them what to do are typically called programmers. They write the programs (lists of instructions) that make computers act in a certain way, test the programs, debug the programs (correct errors), maintain and update the programs, and may even write the documentation (instructions on how to use a program or computer system effectively).

In the past systems analysts designed software programs to meet specific needs, and programmers had the task of writing programs to fill those needs. Today there is a blurring of these responsibilities and job titles, and many individuals are performing both tasks, especially in smaller firms.

Professional programmers often have bachelor's or master's degrees in computer science. Nevertheless, many excellent programmers have little or no formal instruction in programming. For example, many computer buffs regularly enjoy writing programs for their own computers. To gain professional expertise, they will have to learn how computer circuits are structured and should have a strong background in several programming languages. These languages have a fixed vocabulary and a set of rules that allow programmers to create instructions for a computer to follow. There are numerous programming languages, and no one language meets the needs of all programmers.

Being a programmer requires an ability to pay extraordinary attention to detail. For example, just omitting a comma in an instruction can cause a system to fail. Programmers also must be able to think logically and concentrate on a task for long periods. In addition, they need to have stamina. It is not unusual for programmers to work eighty-hour weeks and go for days without much sleep when they are trying to meet deadlines. Creativity is also an asset for programmers who must find unusual solutions to resolve difficult problems. And, of course, programmers must stay current on programming languages as well as the continual changes in technology.

On the job, programmers may work alone or be part of a group. They may be responsible for creating an entire program or just a segment of a program. It may take just a few minutes to write a program, or it may take years.

Most computer professionals begin their careers as programmers. You can divide programmers into two basic groups: systems programmers and applications programmers. Some might want to add other groups for those who work in very specialized programming areas.

Working as a Systems Programmer

Systems programmers design and develop all the software used to operate a computer system. They also are involved in installing, debugging, and maintaining systems software once it is installed. You will find most systems programmers working for computer vendors, from giants such as IBM to small start-ups. The trend toward standardization of operating systems has now made it possible for systems programmers to move more easily from working with one vendor to another. Formerly, most vendors tended to have their own operating systems making it essential for programmers to learn a new system when they switched jobs. A few systems programmers work at end-user organizations where they support applications programming, make evaluations of hardware and software, and modify existing software. They also develop programming standards.

CAREER PATH   Most systems programmers begin as junior or trainee programmers and receive considerable direction from project managers or team leaders. They typically advance to programmers, who receive less supervision, and then to senior systems programmers, who work independently. They can advance to project leader in charge of heading a team of programmers and to manager of operating systems with the responsibility or directing all activities of the department. The number of levels on the career path of a systems programmer depends on the size of the organization. Systems programmers do have a variety of career choices. Some elect to go into management, some choose to remain in programming, and others may prefer to move into systems analysis.

EDUCATION   Systems programmers will usually have degrees in computer science. They also need to have a good knowledge of assembly language, which is used in operating-systems programs. In addition, they should understand computer architecture, which is the overall design by which the individual hardware components of a computer system are interrelated.

Working as an Applications Programmer

Applications programmers write programs that tell computers how to perform specific tasks from billing customers to sending the shuttle into space. They turn design specifications into computer code, which means putting the steps necessary to execute a program in a programmable language. Applications programmers also debug and test programs and may write documentation. All of their work is user oriented rather than system oriented, like the work of systems programmers. And you will find them at work in a variety of places. They may be creating software at Lotus Development Corporation, WordPerfect Corporation, a grocery chain, banks, universities, research centers, and NASA; or they may be working by themselves at a mountaintop retreat. Wherever they are, you will frequently find them working as part of a team made up of sales and marketing, documentation, training, and quality control people to create a product. You also will find them in tense, pressure-packed situations trying to meet deadlines to finish a program on time.

Formerly applications programmers would develop systems from the designs of systems analysts. Now they work more closely with the users of their programs and often take over the design function as well. Thus, they may more appropriately be called programmer/analysts or software engineers.

CAREER PATH Applications programmers work in two distinct areas: business applications and scientific or engineering applications. The career path in either area is similar to that of systems programmers. Applications programmers also begin as junior or trainee programmers, then advance to programmer, to senior programmer, to project leader, and on to manager of applications

programmers. As for systems programmers, the number of inter-
mediate steps in their career paths depends on the size of the
organization for which they work. Applications programmers
may change career direction and become systems programmers
or systems analysts. Because applications programming is often
the first job for those who are interested in information systems,
many applications programmers will ultimately take managerial
positions.

EDUCATION   Applications programmers do not always have college degrees. There are high school students working as programmers. However, most applications programmers are college
graduates. Those specializing in scientific or engineering applications need to have strong backgrounds in those subject areas.
Applications programmers also need to be proficient in a high-
level programming language such as C.

Developing the Programs You Use— A Programmer's Story

When Fred Parsons sits down at a computer to program, he sees
himself as an artist with the monitor his canvas and the keyboard
his brush. Fred is a programmer at Timeworks, Inc., which
produces education and productivity software. The company is
one of the top one hundred producers of software in the United
States and has won awards for several programs.

As an undergraduate, Fred took only one computer course, a
course in FORTRAN, and really enjoyed the programming part
of the course. After graduating from college, he did not become
a programmer but was a high school teacher for four years. The
uncertain future in being a teacher with so many layoffs occurring
in his area convinced Fred to go back to college and work for a
master's degree in computer science. Halfway through the degree

program, he started looking for work and found a job as a programmer/analyst at Timeworks, Inc., where he has remained ever since. His first job was to write demos of programs the company was selling, so customers could see the actual screens from these programs in smaller software stores. It was a compiled BASIC program. Fred was pleased with this assignment. The project manager would tell Fred what he would like to see and whether the job was going according to specifications. He also helped Fred with programming problems.

By his next assignment, Fred had begun to climb up the programmer career ladder. He was the only programmer on a team that included a writer, a packager, and people from marketing and advertising. All worked together under the direction of a project manager to produce a data base program. The company told Fred what type of program he was to create and left some things to his discretion. He had learned about data bases in his graduate school courses in computer science but had to teach himself the programming language he used to create the data base program. Logic and discipline from his undergraduate programming course and five or six graduate-level programming courses helped make this endeavor easier. Fred's experience clearly shows how helpful computer science courses can be to programmers in their work.

On the data base project, Fred worked on the coding part alone and even did some of the design work. Coding involves writing down every single instruction the computer is to perform in a given computer language. For example, if a computer were to ask a question, it might take from one to one thousand instructions to make it ask the question in a user-friendly fashion. In coding, you write down certain key words or variables and mathematical equations; then a compiler turns your language into actual instructions for the computer in a language the computer can understand.

Once Fred's company saw that he could come up with ideas (programmers must be creative) and specifications, he advanced to the position of project manager and reported to the director of research and development. At one time, he was supervising four projects at once. Fortunately, the deadlines for the programs were staggered. As far as his future goes, Fred says that programming is habit-forming—you get hooked on it—so he likes the idea of continuing to program. He also likes the idea of being in management as he is able to express his opinion more as well as work with people. In any case, Fred says he never gets bored working in programming as the possibilities are endless, and there is always new technology to learn. For example, he learned the high-level language C, which he is using in his current project, by simply buying a book and going on from there. Fred strongly believes that there will always be a need for programmers. He is especially glad to have a job creating software for a software company rather than working for an organization where he might only be modifying old programs.

Debugging Programs to Make Them Work

Being a computer buff may run in some families. Rob Needham's father and grandfather have worked with computers most of their lives, and he seems to be following in their footsteps. While Rob was attending college and working as a volunteer at a supplemental food program, a program secretary asked him to look at a computer program that was giving her trouble. He looked at the program, saw where it failed, and contacted the program's developer at a local firm. After many conversations with the owner of the small company, CK Computer Consultants, Rob was offered a part-time job doing data entry work. This led to his present position as a quality control specialist. The company specializes in software applications in the medical field. It is a very small firm with just four employees: the owner, a secretary, a part-time programmer, and Rob.

Rob's basic job is to make the company's programs bulletproof. Anytime a modification is made in one of the firm's programs, he has to check that program in a variety of ways to make sure that it still works properly and doesn't fail. When a new program is developed, he tries to "destroy" it (make it fail), and many times he succeeds. For example, in one program, patients were identified by their social security numbers or machine-generated numbers. Rob discovered that the same number could be given to more than one patient, which would have quickly corrupted the data. After he found this flaw, he described how he caused it and offered a solution. The owner, who designs all the programs, corrected the flaw, and Rob then retested the solution in several other ways. He tries to recreate errors by going through a different path. The process continues until Rob can no longer find any errors. In an eight-hour day, his error sheet may list as many as fifty or sixty errors to be corrected. Rob discovers far more errors in new programs than in existing programs that are being modified for new customers.

Because the company is small, Rob also does general office work and data-entry work for the company or the purchasers of the company's programs. When he works outside the office doing data-entry work, he introduces the workplace staff to his company's program. At the same time, he also may find errors in the program. Rob says that he can test a program seven ways only to discover that the customers are using it in an eighth way. For example, he found out that individuals switching from typewriters to computer keyboards often retain the habit of leaving their hand on the space bar, which can generate errors all over the place. The company's program had to be corrected so that more than three hits of the space bar would not be acknowledged.

Rob is largely a self-taught computer buff, although he has had courses in writing programs in BASIC and FORTRAN plus a course in WordPerfect. He is fascinated by computers and would like to continue debugging programs, as well as get into programming. Rob is working toward that goal by constantly reading computer publications and working closely with his employer.

Documenting Software Programs

When you want to know how to compute averages on your software spreadsheet program, you can easily find the answer by consulting your user manual. Programmers at end-user organizations use technical manuals when they are customizing programs to interface with their system. Installers use manuals when they are implementing a system. All of these manuals are written by technical writers who are skilled writers with a solid knowledge of computers and how they work.

Although Betsy Morris graduated from college with a major in psychology, she has spent most of her career writing about how to use computers and training others to use them. In her first job with a start-up electronics company, she worked in production control buying parts and making sure they would arrive when needed. Then the company brought in a new software system to organize production, and Betsy turned into a computer buff. She became quite expert at using the mainframe production software and soon was putting together manuals on using the computer and holding training classes. This led to a full-time job as an engineering support specialist, which also entailed preparing materials for computer courses and writing a newsletter on the implementation of the new computer software.

After moving to a new town, Betsy answered a newspaper ad seeking someone to do technical writing and user support and was immediately hired for this position at a heavy-construction company. The company had several programmers who developed programs geared to the needs of the engineers and office staff in the firm. Betsy wrote manuals for the users and trained them to use the applications programs. She also was involved in selecting software and computers.

After a move across the country, Betsy made a decision to concentrate on technical writing in her next job. Although she liked to do support work, she felt it was difficult to be good in both areas as there were so many new technological developments to learn. Once more she found a job through a newspaper ad, this time as a technical writer for a software house producing very complex programs in the financial area. The programs were sold to large institutions such as banks and insurance companies. The learning curve has been very steep at this job because Betsy has had to learn not only about how each new program works but also about the companies for whom she writes the manuals.

As a technical writer, Betsy is usually working on manuals for two or more software programs at one time. The point at which she gets involved with a project depends on the project manager and her other commitments. If she is rushing to meet a deadline or has two or three manuals going at once, she cannot get involved until her schedule clears. Ideally she is brought in during the design phase and asked for input, but she often joins a project when this phase is completed. Because documentation has to be delivered a few days after an organization receives a new software program, Betsy is always busy writing the user manual as the programmers are creating the program. She has to work closely with the programmers to get the information she needs for the manuals. Normally, the user, technical, and installation manuals are written by the same technical writer. The user manual is produced first, and the technical manual is finished next because the programmers are always making changes until the program is shipped to clients. Installation manuals, which are done last, are not written for all programs since some programs are so technical that they must be installed by her company.

Betsy wants to remain a technical writer because she truly enjoys the challenge of this work. She describes a good technical writer as an individual who is an excellent writer first and who also understands what he or she is writing about. Betsy sees no lessening in the demand for technical writers, but she does see a tendency in many firms to use contract writers when they need them rather than having a large staff of in-house writers.

A Software Products Manager

Companies that make computers also make or buy systems software. Mike Tognoli is one of Hewlett-Packard's many product managers. Once he is assigned a new software product, a team is put together and a business plan is developed. His team will negotiate with a number of different groups in Hewlett-Packard. For example, Mike must make sure that the new software is compatible with the systems on which it is designed to run. He also works with the group signing contracts with customers. The product must be marketed, which includes pricing and packaging. And, of course, it must be shipped to customers. In addition Mike is concerned about service and maintenance of the product. This area is rather like a new car warranty, as the company will fix problems with the software. Mike also spends time updating customers on the product.

Positions as product managers are usually held by individuals who have some business background. Mike says that managers tend to have or are working towards their M.B.A.'s. Besides having his M.B.A., Mike has work experience as a financial analyst, a marketing manager, and an integrated circuit buyer. The next step up the career ladder for product managers is to fully manage a larger group, rather than a product.

Training People to Use Software Programs

When Ellen Leeb went to work at NeXT Inc., she was not a computer buff but a college graduate with a journalism major looking for a job. She took a job as a receptionist, promising herself to stay at that position only for a year as she looked for other job possibilities in the company. By networking with employees, she discovered an opening for a publications assistant in the software department and was hired for this position proving that taking an entry-level job can lead to future job opportunities.

As a publications assistant, Ellen oversaw the production of three user and eight technical documentation books. Her job was to coordinate the work of technical writers and graphic artists in producing the books. She also worked on having the books localized, which means translating them into different languages in such a way that they fit appropriately into the culture and business strategies of other countries. After SW Publications acquired the training department, Ellen became involved with the production of training manuals as well as all the arrangements for training sessions for users and outside developers. Recently she was promoted to a position in training where, in addition to overseeing the production of training manuals, she also manages groups of trainers.

In creating and producing software as well as hardware, many people are needed to handle administrative tasks. Ellen truly enjoys being involved in the training of users and developers and appreciates the special atmosphere of the NeXT corporation, which respects everyone's individual work ethic. The company has no set hours and operates on a "just-get-the-job-done" philosophy, which makes for a very dedicated staff who really works hard.

Selling Software in a Retail Store

Enter a store jammed with customers searching for just the right software program to solve a business problem, learn something new, or entertain themselves, and you have entered the software retail store managed by Jennifer Frohlinger. She works for Egghead Software, one of the fastest growing companies in the computer industry. Although Egghead was only founded in 1984, it now has more than 205 stores and nearly 2000 employees.

After graduation from Columbia University, Jennifer worked in sales at a brokerage house and then sold vocational training courses. Meanwhile she picked up mainstream information about computers from her aunt, who worked in the industry, and became sufficiently intrigued by computers to take a course in PASCAL. Her real entrance into the computer age occurred, however, when she started to take a graduate program in entrepreneurial design. Not only did she learn the program material on the computer, she also did her homework on the computer.

Jennifer's next job was with Microsoft, where she worked as a support person for account representatives. Her task was to research companies to find out what software they were using and to determine what their software requirements were. She tried to find out how Microsoft could help a company so that the Microsoft salespeople were knowledgeable when they called. Just preparing for the job interview was a challenging task, as she had to spend ten hours a day learning programs so she could give a demonstration. She was successful because she had interviewed program users and knew what they wanted. Her first six months at Microsoft were overwhelming, since she had so much to learn. Jennifer was working eighty hours a week and considered forty hours just part-time work.

A move across the country resulted in Jennifer working briefly in medical software sales. Then, after a short stint as a headhunter, she decided to return to the computer industry. Jennifer also loves to do saleswork, so she walked into an Egghead store and inquired about obtaining a sales position. This store did not have any openings but sent her to another store where she was hired as a full-time sales associate. Being a sales associate required that she become acquainted with software programs and what they did. She accomplished this by doing considerable reading of industry trade publications, watching demonstrations by representatives, and participating in specialized training courses developed by Egghead. The key to her success as a sales associate was finding out what her customers truly needed and giving them immediate answers to their questions. When Jennifer required more information, she would either call the manufacturer or open a demo and read the material. Her expertise as a sales associate led to Jennifer becoming an assistant manager and then a manager of an Egghead store.

Jennifer manages her store as if she owns it. She is responsible for everything in the store including hiring and training staff, handling customer problems, and providing financial accountability. In addition she orders software, sees that merchandise is attractively displayed, and sells software. In the future Jennifer would like to incorporate the skills she developed as a salesperson at an Egghead retail store with her interest in computers by obtaining a job in Egghead's corporate and government sales team, where she would be selling software to Fortune 500 corporations and governmental agencies.

Employment Trends and Salaries

Applications programmers will need to keep abreast of new technologies including the wide array of computer-aided software engineering (CASE) tools. Considerable demand now exists for applications programmers who have knowledge of workstation technologies. Software companies are currently focusing on providing more service, which means the areas of technical support and quality control will expand.

The fantastic increase in the number of personal computers has created a demand for systems programmers able to work with networks of small computers. Furthermore computer vendors continue to need systems programmers to work on new operating systems and revise existing systems.

Programmer Salaries		
Title	Large Installations[a]	Small Installations[b]
programmer/analyst	$34,000–$46,000	$29,000–$39,000
programmer	$28,500–$35,500	$24,500–$33,000

[a] Large installations generally have staffs of more than 50 and use larger mainframes or multiple minis in stand-alone and/or cluster configurations.

[b] Small installations usually have fewer than 50 staff members and only one mainframe or mid-range system with PC-server and LAN connections.

Excerpted with permission from Robert Half International Inc., P.O. Box 33597, Kansas City, MO 64120.

CHAPTER FOUR

Providing Computer Services

A s the use of computers in homes, offices, factories, businesses, the government, and other organizations continues to grow, the need for computer services expands. And fortunately for computer buffs, this means an ever-increasing number of jobs for computer professionals. There are jobs for programmers, systems analysts, systems integrators, data base experts, information systems managers, word processors, data-entry clerks, project managers, and computer operators within the computer services segment of the computer industry.

Professional Services

Large organizations have information systems departments that oversee the operation of their computer systems. Nevertheless, most organizations will probably use outside professional services at times. They may need help in such things as selecting new equipment, networking existing equipment, setting up a disaster recovery program, or creating a new program. Organizations with a small staff of computer professionals will use outside professional services for designing and implementing systems, customizing software, training staff, and maintaining equipment. There is also a trend at present for organizations, large and small, to have service companies handle all or a great part of their information systems work. This is called *outsourcing*.

Service companies vary in the number of services they offer. The most important service today is systems integration. This involves planning, designing, and implementing of computer systems and networks. While some service companies are quite large, there are also a great number of individuals providing these services—many only working part-time.

A Systems Integrator

Jim Horio works part-time as a systems integrator at TJ and K Incorporated, the company he owns with his partner Carl Lindke. When the two established the company, Jim knew a lot about accounting and Carl was an expert programmer who had work experience as a systems engineer with IBM. Jim swiftly learned how to program with help from Carl by working on the S/32 computer in his apartment. Many of their company's clients come from referrals by people they know who work at CPA firms. Their clients (small to midsized companies) are looking for new computer systems or to upgrade their current systems. Jim and Carl will analyze a client's needs, determine hardware and software needed, and put the system together so it works. They also write the software program.

Jim and Carl are telecommunications specialists, a skill which is in high demand today. Much of their current work involves putting in telephone switches. They provide custom programming services to integrate telephone technology into computer applications programming. The two write programs that allow telephones to talk to computers. In addition, they sell Prentice Hall Legal Practice Management software solutions to legal firms. Then they do custom programming to adapt the software to individual firms and integrate legal applications with telephony. Jim and Carl also have written their own application program called JD Calltrack, which Prentice Hall Legal Practice Management will market for them.

When they first started their firm, both Jim and Carl worked full-time at it. Then the emergence of the PC changed the nature of their work, and both took other jobs and did TJ and K work in the evenings and on weekends. Because both are confirmed computer buffs willing to spend most of their free time doing company work, they have been successful. In the future, they see TJ and K taking more of their time as they sell and install more Calltrack systems and get more of the legal market.

Processing Services

Today's organizations have to process vast numbers of transactions and considerable data. They must handle payrolls, insurance claims, inventory, and numerous tax forms as well as perform many record-keeping functions. Some of these chores are routine while others are large-volume, one-time projects. Even companies with large information systems departments are now having much of their large-volume transaction and data work done by processing services. Typically these services will use their own hardware and software. Processing services offer computer buffs such jobs as programmers, project managers, computer operators, and data-entry clerks. They also employ numerous managers and salespeople.

A Data Processing and Accounting Services Company

DPAS started out as a small data-entry shop in 1931. It has grown into a large data processing and accounting services firm with a main office in San Francisco and three branch offices. The firm has from 175 to 500 employees depending on processing needs. Many of these individuals are actively working with the company's basic computer equipment of forty to fifty networked PCs and three S/38s. The company provides a wide variety of services; smaller companies might only handle one type of service. By looking at some of the many services that DPAS provides, you can get a better idea of exactly what processing services these companies offer as well as the types of positions available for computer buffs.

Tax Reporting   The federal government requires companies issuing more than 50 1099s or 250 W-2s to report them on magnetic tape. DPAS puts tax information on magnetic tape and provides firms with a duplicate tape as well as a printout of the contents.

Inventory   DPAS does customized inventory processing using custom programming to give retailers the output they need.

Data Entry   DPAS uses on-site programmers to customize each data-entry project. The company has over 190 key stations for fast, accurate data entry and quick turnaround.

Processing Services   DPAS processing services include transactional batch processing for large banks; large-volume, one-time projects; surveys; payment processing; and product registration plus many other services.

Order Processing and Fulfillment   DPAS handles the mail and telephone order business of firms. Every order from arrival through delivery is tracked by computer.

Direct Marketing Support Services   DPAS supports customers' direct marketing programs through these services: data entry of customer names, response documents, orders, and registration forms; label production; list compilation and maintenance; and order processing.

John Brown is currently chief operating officer of DPAS. He started with the company as a computer operator, became a programmer and project manager, and then managed project managers. John continued climbing the DPAS company ladder advancing from general manager to president of a division and on to his present position. Career stories like John's illustrate how entry-level positions can lead to top management positions.

Information Services

Information services collect related information about a topic, organize it in a useful manner, store it in large data bases, and provide on-line or off-line access to the information. This information usually can be accessed by computer twenty-four hours a day from wherever you are. The almost unquenchable thirst of businesses as well as individuals for information ensures the continued growth of this sector of computer services.

Information services may provide information on hundreds of topics or just a specialized topic. You can access information on such common topics as:

stock quotations

corporate profiles

weather

current news stories

encyclopedia articles

market trends

business news

travel services

sports updates

movie reviews

In addition there are data bases with information designed for specific professions. Doctors now find out about new drugs and treatments by accessing medical data bases. And lawyers are more likely to research case law through a legal data base service than traditional law books.

Computer buffs can find jobs in many areas in information services. There is a need for those interested in software and hardware to improve the technology in creating and distributing information. Individuals with data base management skills especially will be needed as the demand for information continues to increase.

A Small Information Service

Quite often when people think of information services, they think of industry giants such as Prodigy, CompuServe, Dialog, and Dow Jones. There are many smaller information services that provide information for a particular customer niche. One of those services is the Indiana College Placement and Assessment Center (ICPAC). The mission of ICPAC, which was created by the state of Indiana, is to inform, encourage, and support the education and career development of the people of the state. During the school year, ICPAC mails fifteen communications to the homes of students in grades nine through twelve. In addition ICPAC has a free computer resource network—PLAN—which has information about schools, majors, careers, financial aid, and other topics to help students plan their futures. The network is linked to high schools, postsecondary institutions, public libraries, and other state organizations. Both the mailed communications and the computer resource network require the creation and management of data bases.

Jack Schmit, the associate director for research and development, manages the ICPAC data bases with the help of a data base services specialist and four staff members who work part-time in this area. The data base management system originally was created by an outside consultant, who then adapted the system to meet ICPAC's needs. As data base administrator of the PLAN network, Jack's duties include:

- deciding who will have access to the system
- setting up accounts for users including the assignment of passwords
- monitoring the use of the system by individual accounts to ascertain whether an account needs access
- deciding what information should be in data bases
- updating and maintaining information in the data base
- creating new information for the data base
- marketing the data base
- being responsible for software development for the program

In managing the mailings data base, Jack has to organize the records for about 250,000 high school students and their families. This involves obtaining the students' addresses and grade levels and entering the information in the system.

Jack has worked with ICPAC almost from the day it started. He is not formally trained in data base management but has learned through doing. Jack, however, is very knowledgeable about education, as he holds a doctorate in this subject. Being a data base administrator requires more than computer expertise; it also requires a solid knowledge of what information should be in the data base.

CHAPTER FIVE

Solving Users' Problems
The Job of Systems Analysts

W ho are systems analysts? They are the key people around whom the computer systems of banks, insurance companies, consulting firms, financial services, manufacturers, government agencies, and computer companies revolve. They perform three different functions in their job. First of all, systems analysts are people-persons who work with users to find out what information the users expect the computer to generate. Systems analysts are also investigators who gather facts about existing systems and then analyze them to determine the effectiveness of current processing methods and procedures. Finally, they are architects who plan and design new systems, recommend changes to existing systems, and participate in implementing these changes. Being able to handle the three distinctly different roles of a systems analyst requires certain characteristics. If becoming a systems analyst interests you, take this quiz to see if you have most of the requisite traits.

Personality
Are you self-motivated and creative?

Can you work equally well with technical personnel and those with little or no computer background?

Can you handle a number of tasks simultaneously?

Do you have the ability to concentrate and pay close attention to detail?

Are you able to think logically?

Skills

Are you interested in a wide range of subjects?

Can you communicate effectively both orally and in writing?

Do you possess the ability to coordinate activities among many levels in an organization?

Do you have good organization skills?

Do you have a broad knowledge of computer systems?

Are you familiar with programming languages?

Are you a college graduate?

Do you have an analytical mind?

Are you self-disciplined and self-directed?

Are you able to work for long periods with few tangible results?

Do you enjoy attending meetings?

Are you willing to write numerous reports with little accomplishment?

If you answered "yes" to most of these questions, you probably possess the personal qualities and skills to become a successful systems analyst. Your work will be with systems. A computer system is made up of people, machines, programs, and procedures all organized to accomplish a certain task. Organizations have systems because a system is an orderly way to get things done. For example, colleges have systems to register students in the classes they want. These systems have such components as registration forms filled in by the students, lists of available classes, registration personnel, and computer programs.

How Systems Analysts Work

Whether your task as a systems analyst is to create a brand-new registration procedure for a college or to improve the system for regulating the air temperature inside the space shuttle, your project will usually have six phases. How many systems analysts will be involved in developing and implementing a new system and what their individual roles will be naturally depend on the complexity of the system as well as the analysts' expertise.

THE PRELIMINARY INVESTIGATION   is simply a brief study of the problem to find out if it warrants further investigation. The systems analyst primarily handles this phase through personal interviews with people who have knowledge of the problem as well as the system being studied. This phase is usually quite brief. At its conclusion, systems analysts usually give management a report of just a few pages telling what they found and giving their recommendations.

THE SYSTEMS ANALYSIS   phase involves gathering and analyzing data. Systems analysts gather data from interviews, written documents, questionnaires, and personal observations. This phase takes a lot of legwork and time and can be quite expensive. Once all the data have been gathered, it is time to analyze them using such tools as organization charts, data-flow diagrams, grid charts, data dictionaries, and decision logic tables. The final step is to make a report to management that details what problems were found, gives possible solutions, and recommends what the next step should be.

THE SYSTEMS DESIGN   phase involves the planning and development of the systems operation. Systems analysts begin this phase by finding out exactly what information must be produced by the system (output). Once they know what the desired output is, they have to determine what is required to produce it (input), how the data will be stored, and how the system will operate to produce the desired information. An important part of this phase is to develop system controls to ensure the data are input, processed, and output correctly. This phase concludes with a detailed presentation of the system to management and users and, perhaps, with approval to begin developing the system.

THE SYSTEMS DEVELOPMENT   phase begins with the scheduling of all the activities that have to be performed. Then design specifications have to be prepared for all the programming that will be done including the selection of the programming language. After the programs have been written, the next step involves testing to see if all the programs work together satisfactorily. Finally, documentation is required to describe the programs for operations personnel and users of the system.

THE SYSTEMS IMPLEMENTATION AND EVALUATION   phase indicates that the system is ready to operate. The reliability of the system must be tested and necessary modifications made. In addition, there must be a changeover from the old system to the new which involves training personnel. Furthermore, systems analysts must evaluate whether everything is working as planned.

THE SYSTEMS MAINTENANCE   phase begins when the development process is concluded. Changes have to be made to correct errors, give the system additional capability, or react to new needs of the users.

Working as a Systems Analyst

It helps to have a little bit of Sherlock Holmes in you in order to be a successful systems analyst. You must investigate until you find out exactly what an end user really needs, and many end users are not able to express precisely their computer needs. You also must be a teacher willing to help reluctant users learn to feel comfortable with computers and computer technology. Furthermore, you must realize that you are changing a familiar system and may find some end users are reluctant or even antagonistic about these changes. Tact is absolutely essential in working with these people. Computer analysts must wear many hats as they work on devising new systems or modifying older ones. Besides interacting with people, they must be skilled professionals who can choose the correct hardware and software and design systems that meet the needs of an organization and its end users.

A Systems Analyst at a University

John Boyer is currently a systems analyst working in the controller's office at Ohio State University. His close association with the university began with his undergraduate studies there in computer science. After graduation, he worked for four years in the university's office of planning, followed by three years in the budget office. Along the way, he received his M.B.A. from Ohio State University. Except for a brief stint with another organization, John has always worked at the university.

John began his career at the university as a programmer, which is the typical starting point on the career path of many systems analysts. His programming experience was all project-oriented as he worked on developing "what if" models. The purpose of these models was to help determine various outcomes when given a particular set of assumptions. On one project he devised "what if" models for student attrition rates and an enrollment projection program for use on a microcomputer. Originally, the model only ran on a mainframe, but today it takes only seconds to run interactively on the microcomputer. Because the models that John developed in the office of planning studies were management decision-making tools, they had to be extremely accurate. He also developed small, project-oriented systems that solved clear-cut problems given to him by university officials. John had to develop applications quickly for these problems, because the officials wanted the information almost at once to implement their ideas.

After an absence of a year and a half from the university, John returned as a systems analyst 3 assigned to the controller's office. At Ohio State systems analysts work for different departments in addition to a centralized computer facility. Systems analyst 3 is the highest position on the systems analyst career path, with systems analyst 1 being the entry-level position. John typically works on two or more projects at the same time. His major project right now is for the university accounting department. The accounting system handles over 750,000 transactions a month for 300 different departments having annual expenditures exceeding $1.3 billion. All the departments need to get information into the accounting system. At present this is accomplished by having department staff fill out forms on carbon paper, which then are sent from office to office gathering the necessary signatures so they can be put into the university accounting system. John's project goal is to design a transaction management system so that all three hundred user departments will have access to the computer system of the accounting department, thus eliminating forms being passed from office to office. Each user will be able to directly input the information into the system, and then the system will electronically route the form to each appropriate office until all the signatures have been collected. Finally, the form will be directly transmitted into the university accounting system. John is currently in the design phase of this project. Much of his time is being spent meeting with users' groups.

John enjoys the challenges of being a systems analyst and the variety in his work. He especially likes talking to end users, because the systems he designs will play a very important role in their work. As far as the future is concerned, he believes that successful systems analysts will have not only detailed knowledge of systems but also of special application areas such as accounting. For that reason, he is currently studying to become a certified public accountant. He has found the salary as an analyst to be excellent; however, because the computer operation is so decentralized at Ohio State University, he does not believe that as an analyst he can climb the career ladder any higher. Ultimately, he would like to move into the area of finance, where greater opportunities for advancement exist.

John wants individuals considering careers as systems analysts to realize that the job will frequently require more than a forty-hour workweek. And he believes that individuals interested in being systems analysts also should know that in this job they will not spend *all* of their time writing programs, as some people think. Furthermore, he says you must be able to handle pressure-packed days. Since information systems management has become far more complicated in the past ten years, particularly with data bases becoming more complex, future systems analysts will need to be able to understand and model information. Learning about spreadsheets, data base managers, and word processing and communications packages also will be very useful. John believes that systems analysts need to have a broad base of knowledge in order to solve the problems that come their way.

A Systems Analyst at an Army Finance Center

David Charles is a true computer buff. He says, "The computer has great appeal to me—it enhances me." His interest in computers grew as he saw computers becoming so popular in the workplace and in homes. David truly enjoys spending his leisure time at home on the computer. He handles most of his correspondence using word processing and graphics packages on his PC. And during the bleak winter months, you will find him playing educational games on his computer.

David climbed the career ladder to his present position as a project manager for small systems by progressing though a series of jobs. He started as a basic programmer and subsequently became a programmer/analysts, a section leader, and a department leader. His current job consists primarily of managing a tax input system (PC-based, from external offices to a central site mainframe). He writes procedures for system users, analyzes problems, and advises troubled sites. David also is a team chief responsible for nine systems analysts working in many subject areas within the military pay system.

David believes that as a systems analyst you are more marketable if you have management experience, which also can help you, in some instances, to negotiate a better salary. He likes the opportunities that are open for him in the future, which include either continuing to work for the government or going with a large corporation. His advice for future systems analysts is to get a sound educational background and be careful not to become overspecialized in one area as technology is constantly changing.

Education Requirements for Systems Analysts

At present there is no course of study that will completely prepare an individual to become a systems analyst, because employers have such different requirements. Not only are they seeking college graduates with degrees in some aspect of computer science, they also want their successful job candidates to have coursework related either to business or to the area in which they will be working. For example, graduates who have an education background in physical sciences, applied mathematics, or engineering are preferred for work in scientifically oriented organizations. Furthermore, many systems analysts have M.B.A. degrees, which give them the additional expertise in business required for many analyst positions.

If you plan to enter this field, you need to realize that continuous study will be required as technology is advancing so rapidly. This can be accomplished through in-house training, vendor courses, classes, and seminars. It also will be important for you to obtain certification. Certification shows your professional experience. Certified systems professionals have five years of experience as an analyst and have passed a core examination and two additional tests in two specialty areas. You can find out more about certification by contacting the Institute for the Certification of Computer Professionals, 2200 East Devon Avenue, Suite 268, Des Plaines, Illinois 60018.

Climbing the Career Ladder

Almost all systems analysts begin their careers as programmers. Then they will advance to programmer/analysts or senior programmers before being advanced to systems analysts. The following chart shows some of the positions on a systems analyst's career path. More managerial responsibility occurs at each higher level. Many analysts advance into information systems management or senior management in an organization.

Career Path for Systems Analysts
Manager of Systems Analysis
Lead Systems Analyst
Senior Systems Analyst
Systems Analyst ←——————————— Programmer

Employment Trends and Salaries

In 1993, over 400,000 people were employed as systems analysts. They worked for large organizations such as Fortune 500 companies and the federal government. They also worked independently as consultants. Most systems analysts, however, were found in manufacturing, processing, and financial organizations.

Demand remains high for systems analysts as advances in technology continue to lead to new applications for computers. Also, falling prices of both computer hardware and software are enticing smaller organizations to expand the computerization of their operations. In addition, as end users become more aware of the computer's potential, the need for systems analysts will increase. This will be especially true in the areas of office and factory automation, telecommunications technology, and scientific research. Attrition in the field of systems analysis is very small. Individuals leaving this occupation usually transfer to jobs in management or administration.

Because systems analysts typically have several years of work experience before reaching this position, their pay scale is high. The following chart shows the current range of salaries for systems analysts at different levels of an analyst's career path:

Systems Analysts' Salaries		
Title	Large Installations[a]	Small Installations[b]
Senior Project Manager	$55,000–$70,000	
Project Manager	$50,000–$64,000	$41,000–$52,000
Senior Project Leader	$48,000–$61,750	
Project Leader	$44,500–$56,000	$38,000–$47,000
Systems Analyst	$42,000–$52,500	$34,000–$44,000

[a] Large installations generally have staff of more than 50 and use larger mainframes or multiple minis in stand-alone and/or cluster configurations.
[b] Small installations usually have fewer than 50 staff members and only one mainframe or mid-range system with PC-server and LAN connections.

Excerpted with permission from Robert Half International, Inc., P.O. Box 33597, Kansas City, MO 64120.

Running Computer Systems

When the use of computers in organizations first became widespread, large staffs were required to operate the equipment. Many people were needed to input the information on punched cards, mount and remove magnetic tape, and handle the printed output. Preventive maintenance was performed almost on a daily basis by customer engineers sent by the manufacturers. As computers became more sophisticated, smaller operations staffs were able to keep them running. The main reason for the reduction in staff was that input and output activities were being done away from the computer center by end users of the information. Today it is possible for one individual per shift to handle the operation of some computer facilities. Nevertheless, in large computer facilities a sizeable staff is frequently needed. You will find such staff positions as shift supervisors, computer operators, peripheral computer operators, hardware technicians, data-entry staff, and librarians. Although computer operations is one area in which it is possible to get entry-level jobs without specialized training, many staff positions require considerable technical knowledge. Furthermore, because technology is constantly advancing, individuals who work in operations must be willing to develop new skills. Today's equipment is likely to be tomorrow's dinosaur.

One interesting aspect about operations is the possibility of working in shifts or on weekends or even part-time. Since computers at many organizations run twenty-four hours a day seven days a week, there is frequently a need for the operations staff to work around-the-clock.

As organizations come to rely more and more on the information generated by their computers, the importance of the smooth and reliable operation of computer systems increases. It is easy to understand why the Internal Revenue Service, nuclear power plants, transportation systems, airline reservations systems, and many other organizations need a solid performance from their operations staffs.

Working as a Computer Operator

Who are the computer operators? They are the individuals responsible for the operation of computer systems. Computer operators work directly with the computer. They make sure that the equipment is in running order; they mount and remove tapes or disks; and they manage the flow of jobs through the system. Computer operators also handle the difficulties with programs or the hardware for systems users.

The centralized computer department of The Sharper Image has four operators with just one operator working on each shift. According to Bill Needham, who is manager of the operations department of this chain of seventy-four retail outlets, the operators have the following duties:

1. Execute procedures at the right time.

2. Respond to computer generated messages.

3. Print and distribute reports.

4. Clean peripheral equipment.

5. Assist end users with routine operational problems such as not being able to sign on.

6. Add and relocate workstations and printers.

7. Save and restore files as requested by the programmers.

8. Reprint misplaced reports that may be difficult to find.

9. Call supervisor when operators do not know what to do.

10. Assist employees at retail outlets with operational problems related to point-of-sale registers.

Much of the work of these operators is routine and involves following a run-sheet, which tells them what they should be doing each hour.

A Computer Operator at a Large Facility

For the past six years, Bryan Morrison has started his job as a computer operator at midnight when he is locked in a computer room about the size of a basketball court at a large army finance facility. He always finds the room's temperature between fifty-five and sixty-five degrees Fahrenheit in order to dissipate the heat generated by the computers and to control the humidity more easily. Brian brings a solid background in computer skills to his job, as he graduated from college in computer technology. He also used a PC in his prior job with an advertising agency.

During the first ten minutes of Bryan's shift, he meets with the supervisor for a briefing and then has another briefing with the shift that is getting ready to leave. These briefings ensure that Bryan's graveyard shift will be able to handle anything that is going on during the turnover time between shifts. He also finds out which jobs are running, which drives are down, and what problems might occur on his shift. In addition, Bryan is told which messages to watch out for on the computer screen.

There are thirteen people on Bryan's shift: a shift supervisor, a lead computer operator, five operators working on peripheral output, two operators on the AMDAHL system, three operators on the 22/600, and a floater. When Bryan works as an operator on the 22/600, which handles all pay, he has a variety of duties. First he needs to see what work has been started and then update daily retired pay, health professional pay, reserve pay, ROTC pay, and many other categories in the pay system. When a job is done, he puts the tapes on a cart so that they can be stored in the library. As an operator, Bryan's main responsibility is to get a job to run correctly. If there are any errors in the program, he must fix them, if possible. If he is unable to fix an error, he will need to call in a programmer.

Bryan really enjoys his job when he is able to help the system solve a problem. He finds this aspect of his job very challenging. However, when there are no problems and too much slack time, Bryan feels that he is not learning anything about computers. Because computer technology is advancing so rapidly, he says that operators must keep abreast of these changes. He plans to go back to school and learn more computer languages. Ultimately he would like to own a business in which the computer plays a major role.

Supporting Computer Operations

The PCs, printers, telecommunications devices, and other computer equipment found in organizations have to be serviced and maintained. Some organizations will have this work done by outside service organizations. However, many organizations have hardware technicians on their staffs to keep their computer systems up and running smoothly. As the use of computers continues to expand, so does the need for hardware technicians. Beginning technicians usually have some training in electronics or electrical engineering. They typically get their training at vocational and technical schools and junior colleges or from the armed forces. There is also on-the-job training. And as technicians climb their career ladders to more supervisory positions, they usually take specialized courses. Entry-level technicians have salaries in the low $20,000 range, while experienced senior technicians may earn over $40,000.

Technicians need to have good manual dexterity and patience as well as the ability to communicate with computer users. Take the following quiz to see if you possess the skills needed to be a technician:

Do you like to fix and install things?

Are you a good listener?

Can you ask questions to obtain information from others?

Do you enjoy figuring out why something is not working?

Do you have good powers of observation?

Are you able to work under pressure?

Do you enjoy working with tools?

Are you able to handle working with people who are are irate?

Do you have an interest in computers?

Are you willing to keep up-to-date on different systems?

Are you physically strong enough to lift heavy equipment?

Do you enjoy reading? (You will constantly be required to read manuals to update your knowledge).

Having a career as a technician is definitely a hands-on job. You need to enjoy tinkering with equipment and have the persistence to locate and solve users' systems problems.

Supporting the operation of computers is not limited to hardware technicians. Many individuals do the paperwork involved in purchasing, repairing, and maintaining computer systems. In addition, many technicians find themselves doing far more than maintaining and servicing computer equipment, as you will see in the following interview.

Working as a Technical Analyst

Michael Holtz is a technical analyst at the Toledo Hospital. Michael feels good about his job because he is able to save the hospital money. He knows that they are getting his services cheaper than if they were to hire someone outside the hospital to repair computer equipment, as he does far more than computer repair work. Michael took the first step on the career path leading to his present position in 1983 when he applied for a scholarship to the Ohio Council of Private Colleges and Schools. He wanted to enter the computer hardware technology field. Michael received the scholarship and was granted a full ride in the ten-month program except for room and board and the expense of some books.

After graduation, Michael began working at Abacus II, a retail store that not only sells computers but provides technical support to customers. As a bench technician he had the responsibility of taking in CPUs and repairing them. After a year and a half in this slot, he went to a branch store where he was the only person providing the needed support for the customers who purchased equipment from this store. He held this position for a year and then was promoted to head technician at the corporate store where he supervised three technicians. Michael left this position to do on-site computer repair for large corporations that the company serviced. He stayed at this job until he began his present job at the Toledo Hospital.

Michael is the only technical analyst at the hospital. His duties include keeping the hardware running, repairing computers, keeping track of repair costs, purchasing necessary parts, doing paperwork for repairs and purchases, and providing assistance on the operating systems and the software programs. He assists four

systems analysts, which includes giving them his recommendations on new systems they have selected to purchase.

On the day Michael was interviewed for this book, he was
involved in a wide variety of activities. He was doing his weekly
time sheets that show where he has spent his time in the hospital.
He had installed a new printer and moved equipment. Michael
also had spent some time installing another hard drive in a system
that needed more drive space. He then spent two hours with the
systems analysts who brought to his attention the users who will
be adding or upgrading programs.

Michael has always been a tinkerer, and he gains great satis-
faction by being able to keep the hospital computers up and
running through his efforts. He counts the pluses of his particular
job as being able to talk to users and resolve their problems over
the phone. He also likes the work hours and the benefits program
at the hospital. Michael is now contemplating taking a two-year
systems analyst course. Whatever he does in the future will
involve computers, as he is a confirmed computer buff.

Working as a Computer Equipment Analyst

Within the operation of a large computer facility, it is essential
to have staff involved in the selection of computer equipment
and peripherals as well as repair and maintenance. This is Garrett
Zawadsky's job as a computer equipment analyst at a large army
finance facility. Systems analysts tell Garrett what type of new
equipment or peripherals are needed. He then writes up the
specifications. Before new equipment is purchased, he will act as
a point of contact between the systems analysts, users, contrac-
tors, and commercial manufacturers. Once a contract is signed,
he checks to make sure the equipment is received. And during
all this process, he is constantly sitting and working on his PC
to put it together. Another part of his job is going into the data
base to track computer repairs. He also does the paperwork for
repairs.

Garrett became a computer buff shortly after his father gave him his first computer. Within two weeks, he was buying add-ons. Today, he has three computers and is constantly involved in upgrading each one. While reading computer magazines, one of his favorite avocations, he learns more about the latest computer and equipment, which is very helpful in his job, and at the same time dreams of future personal acquisitions.

Garrett did not work in the computer industry immediately after graduating from Purdue University. With his education degree, he did substitute teaching and then entered civil service working first as a clerk/typist and then in army supply at the army finance facility where he now works. About the same time he got his first computer, he also took a job in the facility engineering department, where he started to use the computer at work. Although he was only entering data for a supply catalog, his aptitude for the computer was quickly recognized, and he was sent to a school to learn operator functions. In his next job, he was an actual computer operator working on a mainframe doing backups, taking care of input and output from the system, loading jobs, sending jobs to others, and making sure the computer was running. He held this job for one and one-half years before taking his current job. Many individuals who start as data-entry clerks as Garrett did quickly advance up the computer career ladder in operations.

Although unsure of where his career will take him, Garrett can not imagine having a job where he is not using a computer. One area in which he would like to be involved is the software creation of multimedia type effects.

Working in Data Entry

Data-entry operators are the people who input data into computer systems. They key data into a terminal and see what they have typed on a computer monitor. Data-entry operators may work on a PC or be linked to a computer system. The data are keyed to tape or disk. Demand is always high for data-entry operators. The basic criteria for obtaining a data-entry position are speed and accuracy on the keyboard. Clerical skills such as answering the phone, typing, and filing also may be essential. You can prepare for this position by taking high school or vocational school courses. Use the following quiz to determine if you have the necessary traits to be a successful data-entry operator.

Can you easily follow directions?

Do you mind sitting for an eight-hour day?

Are you able to concentrate in a room with other workers?

Are you able to work with little supervision?

Do you like idea of inputting information into a terminal?

Do you have good keyboarding skills?

Are you able to cope with the pressure of deadlines?

Can you handle working in front of a computer screen all day?

"Yes" answers to most of the questions indicate that you could probably handle working as a data-entry operator. You may begin as a trainee or as a data-entry operator. Advancement in this career path is limited to positions as supervisors who assign work to other data-entry operators and make sure the data-entry department is running smoothly. In the following interviews, you will learn more about the tasks that data-entry operators do and discover that these operators are taking on many additional responsibilities.

Data-Entry Operator for the Federal Government

Teresa Reed knew after taking several computer programming and applications classes in high school that the computer would be her ticket to a job in government service. This turned out to be true as there was a hiring freeze when she applied for a government job and the only position she could get was as a data transcriber. For eight months eight hours a day, Teresa was a key puncher punching documents into a terminal that was recording her input on tape. Although she received on-the-job training, Teresa found it frustrating that she had no knowledge of what she was punching in. She also believed that she was not learning on her job and that her only responsibility was production. In fact, she spent her workdays punching in data and listening to her headset. Being a data transcriber, however, proved to be a good entry position for Teresa as she has become a government accounting technician. She now enjoys her time on the computer because she is uploading files and keeping records on a PC. In addition, Teresa is now working on programs and a variety of other tasks on the PC, all of which she finds very exciting.

Data-Entry Clerk at a Small Business

Kim Reed took only one computer class in high school, a basic programming course, but she has spent the last seven years working exclusively on the computer. On her first computer job with the public defender's office, she spent five hours of her eight-hour day typing legal documents and correspondence. Her on-the-job training was in using Multimate, a word processing program. After two and one-half years in the public defender's office, Kim went to work as a data-entry clerk for a window and door company. The company has five outlet stores selling quality windows and doors and a main office where she works as the company's sole data-entry operator. Kim spends her day working on two different systems: the company system and the factory system.

Kim's workday begins when she receives a printout of all the files that she entered the day before on the factory system. She checks to make sure that the files have come back from the factory the way that she entered them. Kim then goes through all the orders that have been faxed in overnight and makes decisions about any changes that have occurred. At this point, Kim goes into the sales journal in the company file and logs in all jobs, construction types, sales representatives, and amounts of money. The next step in Kim's job is for her to pull up customer files, make any necessary changes in individual files, and create customer files for new jobs. The next file that Kim works on is order maintenance, where she enters order headers and creates documents from the orders listing all products that have been purchased by the customers. After printing everything she has entered in the computer, she staples each printout to the order and gives it to the individual who will write up the orders for the factory system. Kim's work for the morning is now completed.

After lunch, Kim spends the next few hours on the computer working on the factory system. She returns to the order maintenance file, creates order headers, and types in information for the orders needed from the factory. Before Kim leaves the factory system, she prints out all the order data that she has entered and sends the orders by modem to the factory. The final hour in her workday is spent doing additional data-entry work, making phone calls, answering questions, and printing copies of contracts. You clearly can see that Kim's job description as a data-entry operator involves considerable decision making and is not just inputting data.

Kim says that her job has taught her about windows and doors and the importance of the computer to the operation of her company. She enjoys typing and having the same daily routine. Kim says she is good at what she does because she does it every day. Over the years, she has gained speed and accuracy because she knows not only the codes but also the system. Kim accepted a new job with the company in the order department because she wanted the additional mental stimulus of a more demanding job. Once again, an individual has used the job of data-entry clerk to advance her career path.

Working as a Librarian

You probably think that you have heard of everything now! Yes, there really are computer librarians, and you will find them at large computer facilities and information centers. They have the responsibility for classifying, cataloging, and maintaining files and programs that are stored on cards, tapes, disks, diskettes, and other media. And they also make sure that all this material is kept in good condition. Computer librarians store back-up files, combine old files, and even supervise the cleaning of magnetic tapes and disks. Just like other librarians, computer librarians help people locate information, the difference being this information is retrieved from stored master computer files.

Education and Advancement

Computer buffs who want to work on computers do not necessarily need a college degree in computer science. This chapter has shown you a number of entry-level positions that will let you work with computers without spending four years in college. Most of these beginning jobs will offer you some on-the-job training. These jobs are not necessarily dead-end ones, as many will lead to your obtaining other positions working with computers.

CHAPTER SEVEN

Managing Information Systems

The history of information systems is a brief one, going back to the days when systems and procedures departments set up courses of action for the efficient use of paperwork and employees. Today's information systems departments revolve around using the computer to develop and provide information to the staff of organizations from the federal government to your local fast-food restaurant. When organizations first started using computers, they were usually placed in data processing departments and used to handle bookkeeping and inventory functions. These departments were typically run by data processing managers, who were considered technical experts by the senior management who really did not know much about computers or computer applications. At the same time, data processing managers were often inept in communicating to management the more sophisticated ways computers could be used in their organizations. The job of data processing manager was considered to be a dead-end job, not an avenue for advancement to the top management of an organization.

As computers became cheaper and more powerful and as a wide variety of software packages became available, companies started using computers for more than just mundane tasks. Computers were elevated to the realm of running the business of the organizations and managers used them to order shipments, purchase inventory, and make decisions. The position of information systems manager evolved to interface the needs of management for computer information with the rapidly expanding capabilities of computers. And the term "information processing" came to be used for "data processing" in many organizations.

The Job of Information Systems Manager

The manager of information systems has the responsibility of efficiently and effectively directing the operation of the computer systems on which an organization depends, plus providing the employees with the information services they need. A typical information systems manager will have the following job responsibilities:

- keeping abreast of trends and advancements in hardware and software technology
- evaluating new technology for possible use in the organization
- making recommendations for systems improvements
- implementing appropriate back-up and security measures
- making sure that the implementation of new systems is handled in a timely manner
- managing the staff of the information systems department
- staffing and training personnel in the information systems department
- creating a budget for the operation of the systems information department
- assessing the information processing needs of users
- providing specific help to users in operating equipment and obtaining needed information
- consulting with senior management on the organization's information needs

- developing a plan to meet the organization's information needs
- reporting on the status of all information systems operations to senior management
- staying in touch with the activities of the organization
- serving as a buffer between personnel in the information systems department and those outside the department

Where Information Systems Managers Report

Since most organizations introduced computers in the accounting area, it was quite common for managers of information systems to report to the controller or vice-president of finance. In many businesses this is still true today. However, as the importance of information systems to organizations grew, the title of chief information officer (CIO) was created, and information systems managers became part of senior management reporting to the executive vice-president, president, or chief executive officer. When you think of the important role the information systems department plays in the success of such organizations as airlines, banks, insurance companies, and credit card companies, it is quite easy to understand why in many organizations the manager of this department is given senior management status. At the same time, you must realize that in small companies the information systems department may have only one employee.

The Career Path to the Top

As long as computers were primarily used to handle basic processing applications, the manager of the computer department tended to have a technical background. Today, individuals who are selected to head information systems departments may come from either a technical or managerial background. In either case, managers of information systems departments must demonstrate communication skills that enable them to speak to users without overwhelming them with computerese. They also need to have a thorough knowledge of the organization for which they work. Typically, information systems managers have several years of experience working for an organization before they are selected to head an information systems department. A possible path to the top, which includes both technical and managerial experience, is shown in the following chart:

↑ CIO or Top Manager
   Second-Line Manager
   First-Line Manager
   Project Manager
   Systems Analysis Position
   Programming Position

Leading the Information Systems Department of a Fortune 500 Company

International Multifoods, a Fortune 500 company, is a leading processor and distributor of food products to food service, industrial, agricultural, and retail customers in the United States, Canada, and Venezuela. In 1985, Paul Taylor became the organization's vice-president of information services. Paul was very familiar with International Multifoods operations, as he recently was responsible for the performance of one of the company's major operating divisions involving 10 plants, 1,000 employees, and $300 million annual sales. Although Paul had impressive managerial experience, he had absolutely no technical computer background. He did know, however, what he had wanted the corporate information services department to do for the division that he had recently headed. Furthermore, his division had been the company's largest user of the corporate data center resources.

Top management selected Paul for the position of vice-president of information services because the company needed someone to turn around the computer operations. The department had not been meeting users' needs. Thus Paul became the company's first vice-president of information services—a position that reported at first to the office of chief executive and later to the chief financial officer. The corporate data processing department and all related operations were incorporated within the new information services department.

Paul's first task in his new position was to acquire the technical knowledge he needed, which he did by attending classes and seminars. During Paul's six and one-half years managing the information services department, he developed a coherent long-term strategy to ensure that the computer function of the department was meeting the needs of the users and that the corporation was making effective use of the available computer technology resources. Paul oversaw the building of a data center after recommending this major capital expenditure to the board of directors. After the data center was built, a mainframe was installed. Later, the mainframe was shut down, and minicomputers and microcomputers were installed in corporate headquarters. The tasks formerly done by the mainframe were given to an outside service bureau. In addition, Paul decentralized computer operations so that the corporate headquarters' department did not have direct responsibility for the operation and maintenance of the computers of remote operating divisions. These divisions would just send in month-end consolidated financial information. The payroll operation, however, became centralized and was handled by the outside service bureau. By the time Paul left this position to work as an executive with a custom-printing service bureau, he had met the challenge of his assignment by making the computer operations responsive to corporate needs.

The Job of Second-Line Managers

The information systems departments of many organizations have large staffs composed of project managers, programmers, systems analysts, network operators, computer operators, data base analysts, librarians, maintenance workers, and many other employees. Second-line managers are usually in charge of a specific function of the information systems department and the staff supporting that function. They report to the chief information officer and may advance within a few years to this position. Although organizations vary greatly in their number of second-line managers and the functions that they handle, the following chart illustrates some of the positions that you would commonly find at this level. Of course, job titles will differ from organization to organization.

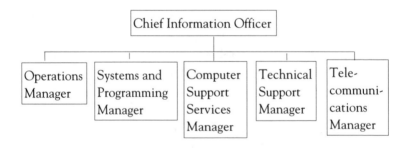

Operations Manager at The Sharper Image

The job of operations manager is to direct and control the operation of all computer and peripheral equipment of an organization. The more essential the operation of computers is to the success of an organization, the more important the position of operations manager becomes. Just imagine the financial cost to an airline if their computers are down for more than a few minutes. Think of the dangerous situation that can occur if computers are not operating properly at nuclear power plants. Contemplate the confusion that occurs at banks, insurance companies, and brokerage houses when their computers are not working.

Bill Needham is the operations manager for the information systems department of The Sharper Image, an upscale retailer with seventy-four outlets. One of the minimum requirements for being an operations manager is having a good knowledge of hardware, software, and operating systems. Bill amply meets these requirements by having almost thirty years of work experience at IBM after graduating from college. His jobs at IBM ranged from education and marketing to systems engineering. While working as a systems engineer at IBM, Bill learned of the opening for an operations manager at The Sharper Image. He decided to take advantage of the early retirement program IBM was offering to become operations manager at The Sharper Image.

In large organizations, operations managers may have many section managers and supervisors reporting to them. At The Sharper Image, Bill has four operators who are responsible for the operation of an IBM AS/400, a midrange computer. Throughout the day and evening, the point-of-sale equipment in the company's outlets sends records of all transactions to the AS/400, plus the time and attendance records of employees. The computer is used to keep track of sales and inventory and to generate a variety of reports for management.

Bill reports to the vice-president of information systems and has responsibilities similar to those of most operations managers. Because his department is small and because of his personal interest in programming, he may spend more hands-on time working on the operation of the computer system than do other managers. Nevertheless, looking at Bill's major responsibilities at The Sharper Image will give you a good idea of the type of work this position entails.

1. Reporting to management on the status of the system, including how close to capacity and speed it is operating

2. Insuring adequate computing capacity is available to handle the work

3. Handling equipment breakdowns so that downtime is minimized

4. Being aware of new technologies and how they apply to his company's system

5. Installing new software to update the system (At times Bill will actually install the software when the operators do not have sufficient expertise.)

6. Putting new equipment in retail outlets, which involves selecting, evaluating, testing, packing, and sending equipment to the stores

7. Negotiating some contracts with outside vendors for maintenance, supplies, and other services such as off-site microfiche storage

8. Staffing the operations department, which includes the hiring, firing, and training of operators

9. Checking operator logs to see if the operators are handling the problems of store personnel correctly

10. Working on disaster preparedness plans

Since the trend in many organizations is to decentralize computer operations and put personal computers on users' desks, the need for operations managers is not likely to increase significantly. Nevertheless, this position remains important in systems management, because downtime can be disastrous for many organizations. Bill, whose interest in computers goes back to his childhood when his father worked for IBM, sees opportunity for advancement in this position either by becoming vice-president of information systems or moving to a company with a larger operations staff.

Programming Manager at Royal Viking Line

Jim Horio is a true computer buff who spends most of his time working with computers. During the day for the past nine years he has worked in the information systems departments of corporations, while at night and on weekends he works at home on projects for his own computer firm. You learned about Jim's company in chapter 4. While working as a contract programmer, Jim saw a newspaper ad for a senior programmer at Royal Viking Line. Lured by the possibility of taking reduced-price cruises, Jim applied for and obtained the job. As a senior programmer, he designed, modified, and wrote new applications programs and worked on user programs for accounting, reservations, and purchasing on two S/38 computers. Within one year Jim was asked to become the programming manager, a second-line management position that reported to the manager of information systems. Besides programming, Jim now had the additional responsibilities of assigning work to the company's six junior and senior programmers, prioritizing assignments, and seeing all the work was done on time—typical responsibilities for a programming manager. Jim's rapid ascent up the information systems career ladder continued as he became a manager of information systems reporting to the vice-president of finance one year later. When Royal Viking Line moved their operations from California to Florida, Jim decided to leave the company. Nevertheless, he had fulfilled his original dream by taking cruises to Alaska, Japan, Europe, and the Caribbean including a working vacation aboard a ship programming an S/34 computer.

Manager of Computer Support Services for a Heavy-Construction Company

In organizations that have many individuals using computers, it is essential to have someone who establishes protocol standards, selects hardware and software, and helps users. At Granite Construction Company, one of the largest heavy-construction companies in the United States, Gail Piper de Mesa handles these responsibilities with the help of three computer support specialists. It is a challenging job since Granite currently has about six hundred PCs with many different kinds of hardware and software, all of which she is trying to network. Soon a new AS/400 computer with all new construction accounting software will be integrated into the system.

The focus of Gail's department is on service to end users. This involves talking users through problems whether they are at headquarters or at a remote office. It also means holding short on-site training sessions for field support representatives at the thirteen branches, as well as having user groups meet at lunch to discuss a topic. And, of course, she also is involved in choosing the hardware and software the users would like to have and seeing that both meet the standards that her company has set. In addition, her department makes sure that new equipment is tested and set up for end users.

Although high school tests revealed that Gail had an aptitude for computers, she was not interested in them at that time and graduated from college with a degree in business administration. In 1972, she joined a major domestic airline working as a passenger service representative and then as a ticket agent where she wrote tickets by hand. When the ticket process was automated, Gail showed such an aptitude for computers that she was soon training outside travel agents and company personnel in how to use computers. After leaving the airline, and when PCs were still a new phenomenon, she worked at a PC company where she sold computers and trained users to operate them. At this job, she learned about personal computers through extensive reading and hands-on experience. Seeing an intriguing ad in the newspaper for someone to evaluate and select PC hardware and software and to set standards led her to her present position with Granite Construction Company.

To have a successful career as a manager of computer support services, Gail believes you must have a fascination for computers. In addition, you must stay focused on the fact that the purpose of computers is to help a business work more productively. No doubt part of her success can be attributed to having such a fabulous memory that she can remember each PC in the company and its software.

More Second-Line Manager Positions

Technical Support Managers have the responsibility of finding new and better ways to use equipment and meet users' needs. In many organizations, the functions of this position are handled by the chief information systems officer or other second-line mangers.

Telecommunications Managers are in charge of the efficient transmission of information for organizations that are geographically dispersed. They also are responsible for the installation and administration of local-area networks.

Security Managers are increasingly being found at the second-management level. Their responsibility is to protect data so that unauthorized persons cannot examine, copy, or alter them.

EDP Managers are now moving away from their traditional location in the accounting area and into information systems. Their function is to supervise the evaluation of computer systems and operational procedures. They identify problem areas and suggest solutions.

Employment Trends and Salaries

Organizations are increasingly placing a greater value on information and expanding their information services. Demand is generally high for individuals to fill top-level positions in information systems management. Organizations are especially looking for managers who can communicate easily with information users and computer users. There is currently a trend in many organizations to decentralize computer operations, and this has resulted in the placement of many highly trained professionals (programmers and systems analysts) under the jurisdiction of department heads rather than top-level information systems managers. In addition, many organizations are "outsourcing," which is having service companies do information systems work formerly done in-house. Decentralization and outsourcing have resulted in many organizations looking for CIOs who can lead information systems departments through these profound changes. These changes also have led to reduced responsibility for some managers, less demand for middle-level managers, and the elimination of some second-level management positions. At the same time, many organizations are actively seeking second-level managers in telecommunications and security, two fast-growing areas in information systems.

Salaries continue to increase for top-level managers of information systems. Those employed at organizations earning the highest revenues tend to have the highest salaries. The following chart shows the current range of salaries for information systems managers:

Information Systems Salaries for Management[a]	
Title	Large Installations
Vice-President	$88,000–$124,000
Director	$74,000–$ 96,000
Senior Manager, Systems & Programming	$63,800–$ 84,550
Manager, Systems & Programming	$58,000–$ 73,000
Manager, Technical Services	$56,000–$ 72,500
Senior Manager, Operations	$49,500–$ 64,750
Manager, Telecommunications	$57,500–$ 73,000

[a]Large installations generally have staffs of more than 50 and use larger mainframes or multiple minis in stand-alone and/or cluster configurations.

Excerpted with permission from Robert Half International Inc., P.O. Box 33597, Kansas City, MO 64120.

CHAPTER EIGHT

Using the Computer in Special Areas

Design, Manufacturing, Animation, Music, and Entertainment

F or many people the computer is a tool used to express their creativity. The architect uses the computer to design buildings. The engineer uses the computer to manufacture cars and planes. Artists and musicians create artistic works on the computer. Graphics specialists generate imaginative special effects for records, movies, and television shows. In a variety of areas, computer buffs can combine their love of the computer with their special talents.

Designing with the Computer

The lower cost and increased power of computers plus the design of sophisticated software packages have led to the common use of computers by designers whether they are architects, engineers, interior designers, or other design specialists. Today's homes, cars, planes, refrigerators, toasters, and furniture all are being designed on the computer. Computer-aided design (CAD) no longer is confined to large corporations such as Ford Motor Company and Boeing Aircraft; you now will find designers in small offices and homes creating designs on powerful PCs. CAD is swiftly replacing designers' drawing boards no matter what they are designing.

To use CAD, the designer can begin by scanning in a design, can use designs or elements of designs in a software-design program, or can use the computer to create a design. Throughout the design process, the designer makes changes by using the command functions of the CAD program. For example, lines can be shortened, lengthened, curved, erased, moved, and so on, and sections of the design can be moved around. The design even can be viewed in 3-D, and a part can be rotated to produce multiple views of it. When the design is finished, it can be stored for reuse or future modification. The design also can be reproduced with a printer or a plotter that uses special pens to draw the design.

A Project Designer Uses CAD

Dawn Jones is a project designer at Hillenbrand Mitsch Design. The firm does space planning, interior design, and facility management for corporate and commercial clients. Hillenbrand Mitsch Design has made a strong commitment to AutoCAD design and has the latest state-of-the-art hardware and software.

Dawn's primary job is tenant space planning. Developers who lease space come to Dawn's firm requesting a space plan for tenants or prospective tenants. First Dawn meets with the tenant to ascertain what the tenant's needs are. Once she knows the tenant's space requirements, she does the actual design work on the computer. Her task is much simpler if the plan of the building is already on CAD. Then she simply finds the plan and proceeds with her space design. If the building plan is not on the computer, she has to go out and measure the building, return to the office, and draw the shell on the computer before she begins her actual space plan. Her completed space plan is shown to the tenant. If the tenant likes her plan and the brokers and leasing agents come to an agreement, Dawn does the construction drawings. This involves such things as showing where walls, restrooms, and storage areas will go. She also does an electrical plan and a finish plan, which has details about wall coverings, carpets, and other finishing touches. All of her plans are done on the computer. After the design is approved by an architect and the necessary permits are obtained, Dawn supervises the construction.

Dawn gained her expertise in designing space while working for her degree in environmental design at Purdue University. Even though she had taught herself CAD in high school by doing the tutorial and reading the manual, she took three CAD courses in college. On the job, Dawn continues to learn more about CAD from her coworkers, who have different specialty areas in which they excel. Dawn would like to continue doing space design work. She sees an ongoing demand for individuals who can do this work, as so many developers want the plans for older buildings to be on CAD. Although the initial drawing of a building is not much quicker with a CAD program than with pencil and drawing board, the CAD plan is more accurate and can be revised quickly.

Civil Engineers Use CAD

Bob Stallard is an assistant project manager for Granite Construction Company. Although Bob primarily uses CAD for developing charts and graphs for presentations, the civil engineers who work for him use it for all their construction drawings of roads and bridges. Most of these engineers are self-taught, because the CAD systems are so complicated. The engineers must do the tutorials and then learn all the options and possibilities by solving real problems.

Bob considers the computer a valuable aid that facilitates the production of drawings. It replaces the normal drafting tools such as pencils, compasses, protractors, and triangles. For example, to draw a circle, the engineer does not use a compass but instead keys in the radius and specific coordinates. By using the computer, the engineers in Bob's department are able to make precise—not just accurate—calculations and drawings. They also are more productive because drawings can be swiftly revised, a process that is both slow and expensive when done on the drawing board. Besides assisting engineers in their drawings, special CAD programs can be used to analyze their designs. CAD helps engineers answer questions: What is the maximum weight a bridge can hold? What is the most efficient design for a cloverleaf? And so forth.

Manufacturing with the Computer

The age of computer-aided manufacturing (CAM) is here. And robots are no longer just starring in movies; they are out in the factory doing innumerable tasks from working in hazardous situations to performing the same job over and over until they are reprogrammed. The automation of factories continues to accelerate as does the demand for professionals who can design and implement these automated systems. Sophisticated CAD/CAM systems work together so that the design is developed on the computer and then sent to computer-aided manufacturing equipment.

An Engineer Works with CAD/CAM

Greg Lyon works at Aircom Metal Products, Inc., which manufactures products through sheet metal fabrication and plastic injection molding. Many of the parts produced by Aircom lend themselves to the use of CAD and CAM. Greg, who is an electrical engineer, spends considerable time designing parts using CAD. He learned how to use the company's system by reading manuals and observing an experienced CAD user.

Greg uses the customer's part drawings and specifications to develop and draw a tool design on the computer. Then a CAM expert, who is a machinist, will determine what aspects of the drawing can be machined by computer-controlled equipment. Because there are many different types of computer-controlled machines hooked directly to the CAD/CAM system, the CAM expert must choose the appropriate piece of equipment. After a machine is chosen, the CAM expert will use the Computer-Aided Machining software to generate the program code, which is sent to the machine via RS-232 serial cable. After minimal setup, a machinist can begin to produce the tooling designed to make parts according to the consumer's specifications.

Not only does Aircom's CAD/CAM system save considerable time and money, it also has increased quality through increased accuracy. In the years prior to CAD/CAM, these same tool designs would have had to be hand drawn and machined using calculations performed by the machinist. Today, with the computer's assistance, a piece can be drawn and machined accurately within four decimal places (.0001 in.), and the software is continually getting better. According to Greg, CAD/CAM is now the cornerstone of manufacturing, and companies must use it to be competitive.

Learning to Be a Graphic Designer

Sarah Craven is a talented artist who always took art courses in high school and college. Now she is attending a postgraduate school to learn graphic design with the ultimate career goal of becoming the art director of an advertising agency. Sarah is not spending her time learning how to draw layouts by hand. Instead, she is constantly working on the computer. In her classes, she is learning how to use several graphics programs; all have different capabilities. Out of class, she is working on her own to master the programs. This involves working with a copywriter to create layouts and designs for print ads. Whatever she can visualize, she can learn to do by manipulating images on her computer screen using a mouse or the keyboard. The only limitation she truly faces is having enough computer memory. Sarah thinks that the more you know about computers, the more likely you are to be hired in today's job market.

Animating with the Computer

Don Bajus is an animator who has made some imaginative commercials that you might have viewed on television. Today he has a new tool—the computer—to help him animate. Don can now animate in 3-D and light the characters and a scene as if they were real. The computer will know where the objects and the characters are as well as their dimensions and will be able to compute where the highlights fall and where to cast the shadows. If a client wants a different camera angle, it is no longer a task requiring weeks of work. Given the proper instructions, the computer will change the camera angle and the lighting automatically.

Don also can use the computer to move characters rather than draw every movement. The computer can make these changes easily compared to cel animation. In cel animation, every movement is a series of drawings made up of key position drawings and in-between drawings. It is the same process in computer animation only the animator moves the character into key positions, such as in a walk where the first key position could have the left leg on the ground and the right leg lifting. The next key position could have the right leg outstretched ready to come down, the left leg moved back, and the body leaning slightly forward. The animator creates all the key positions and then lets the computer do the in-between drawings. This is not an easier task than cel animation because of the difficulty of the dimensional concept. However, having the computer insert the in-between drawings can be timesaving if enough good key positions are done.

And now it is so easy for animators to change colors. Cel animation art is finished on cels with inked/copied lines and paint. When the computer is used, colors are added through a paint program and are affected by the lighting of the scene. Colors in computer animation can be adjusted quickly or changed compared to cel animation. In the new computer 2-D cel painting programs, which are replacing the old way of cel painting, the painting still takes a long time. Nevertheless, the benefits include the capability of adding textures, having constant density shadows and automatic drop shadows, plus the ability to easily change colors. After touching the cursor to the paint palette to pick a new color, the animator then can move the cursor to the area and color to be changed. By pressing the cursor button, every frame in that scene will have the new color in the chosen area. In cel animation, this kind of change would take weeks.

New software programs let Don either draw on paper and then scan the drawing into the computer or draw directly on the screen. From there he can paint the drawing. He also can swiftly move characters in or out of a scene or from the foreground to the background. The backgrounds, foregrounds, and characters are on separate levels, and each level can be moved independently in any direction. This allows for the multiplane effect, as in a zoom-in where multiple levels of objects pick up speed as they move closer to the viewer—something very complicated in cel animation. The more sophisticated animated commercials that you see have computers helping animators like Don produce them.

Computer animation technology is advancing so rapidly that programs are becoming more capable each year. Don, however, feels that programs are still limited in being able to do things in the ways most animators want, as you tend to feel more like a computer technician than an artist when working with them. He believes the main advantage to using computer animation is the ultimate control it gives the animator over each and every item in the scenes and sees very exciting days ahead for animators as the computer programs become more user friendly. In the future, he would like to film his own animated short stories using the emerging technology.

Learning to use a computer for animation can be quite frustrating according to Don. "At first, the computer won't do anything you want," he says. "But as you gain skill, it will do almost whatever you want." Don is glad that he was an animator before he started to use the computer, because he can think beyond the obvious things the computer can do to assist him in his work. Although there are schools teaching computer animation, Don believes that you should become an animator first so you will truly understand what animation is and will realize that the computer is just a tool—an expensive, powerful, and sometimes obstinate "pencil."

Creating Music on the Computer

The computer has invaded the music world. All of Michael Jackson's music is driven and generated by the computer. Even classical musicians are composing on the computer. If Johann Sebastian Bach were alive today, he would probably be composing on the computer. Just as Bach wrote music to order for patrons, Doug Benge and Pete Schmutte, owners of Earmark Music Works, are creating music for clients, usually advertisers. The first step involves talking to the client to find out what the music is to accomplish—the desired mood or image. Then Doug or Pete will use a computer program as they compose a piece of music. The musical notation program transmits what they play on a keyboard to notes that they can see on the computer screen. They remove the floppy disk from the computer, go into their recording studio, put the disk into a computer, and assign their newly composed piece to different synthesizers using two software programs to create the music in a rough form. The client listens to the music, and any necessary changes are made before the final product is recorded. Just as Doug and Pete create music on the computer, so do other musicians throughout the world.

The Marriage of Entertainment and the Computer

Anyone who has seen movies recently is aware of the wide use of computer-generated special effects. In Hollywood, a great number of small firms are emerging to meet the demand of filmmakers who want to put the extra zing of special effects into their movies. Even the giant studios are setting up in-house departments to develop new film techniques. And these techniques can be used to save money. For example, the computer can turn a herd of ten charging bulls into one hundred and can eliminate the need to send actors to exotic locales for filming with just a little work from computer animators. The public's demand for ever more exciting special effects in films will lead to an increasing number of jobs for imaginative computer visual effects and software creators.

Video games are not just appealing to children; adults also spend hours playing these games on computers and on entertainment systems. After all, these games are fun. You can try to beat tennis great Andre Agassi, get a really high Tetrus score, or play *John Madden Football '93*. Besides playing video games, computer buffs can find jobs creating games as well as the hardware to operate them.

Although interactive entertainment is available at the present time in video games and some CD-ROM titles, the age of interactive entertainment is decidedly on the horizon. Interactive media should emerge from being an entertainment niche to having broad-market appeal as the price of interactive systems goes down. You already can enjoy such material as the two CD-ROM discs accompanying the book *From Alice to Ocean: Alone Across the Outback*. Readers can move from hearing the author read of her camel trek across Australia to seeing slides of her adventure. A number of small companies are emerging to produce not only interactive entertainment but also educational materials. In addition, Hollywood studios are entering this arena. Jobs in interactive media are available for computer buffs who are graphic designers, software programmers, and hardware creators as well as those interested in sales, marketing, and management positions.

CHAPTER NINE

Using Computers on the Job

C omputers are rapidly becoming an invaluable aid in almost every job you can think of from astronaut to zookeeper. In fact, there are far more jobs for computer buffs in business, industry, government, and other organizations than with hardware and software companies. These jobs are found in information systems departments and throughout most workplaces. A large concentration of computers and jobs using the computer especially can be found within the financial world of banks, insurance companies, and investment houses. There are also jobs that involve the use of computers in supermarkets, auto repair shops, fire stations, hotels, military facilities, and just about every other workplace.

Much to the delight of computer buffs, almost every job in the twenty-first century will be involved in some way with the computer. This chapter explores the use of the computer in a wide variety of jobs from airline pilot to zoo manager.

A is for Accountant, Actuary, and Airline Pilot

AIRLINE PILOT   Doug Allington is a senior pilot flying a MD-80 for Northwest Airlines. Almost everything he does as a pilot is related in some way to computers. When he bids for routes each month, the computer assigns him and the other pilots to routes by seniority. Upon arriving at the airport for a flight, a clerk punches his employee number in a computer, and the computer gives him a list of the flight crew. Then an hour before takeoff, he receives a computer printout from the flight planning computer listing such things as weather at takeoff, weather at destination, in-route weather, time of trip, routing, winds at cruise altitude, and fuel load. The computer also predicts the plane weight, winds, and temperature at takeoff and gives the optimal runway and takeoff speed. Just before the door closes, the computer will provide him with the final weight. Once the plane is on the runway, Doug takes over and the computer doesn't have much to do. Of course, the computers in the control tower are busy tracking all the planes. A computer aboard the MD-80, which is taking in information from all over the plane, can land the plane in really bad weather. Doug will put information about the heading, course, and speed in this computer. An aircraft communications addressing and reporting computer will send information about arrival and departure times and delays to the airline computer system. This updates the arrival time you see on the screens at the airport. Doug also can use this computer to send in maintenance reports. After he lands, he walks away from the plane as well as its computer support system.

According to Doug, the MD-80 has only a first generation computer system, while the airline's airbuses are the most computerized commercial planes. On the airbuses, the pilot watches six monitors instead of gauges, the plane is steered by a joystick instead of a wheel, and the computer monitors the pilot's actions and will not let pilots exceed the performance limit of the plane. Pilots flying these planes are acting like computer systems managers. Doug says that today's pilots must be computer-wise as computers are beginning to play such an important role in all aspects of flying.

B is for Banker, Broker, and Beautician

BEAUTICIAN   Kenn Williams is a distinguished hairdresser and a computer buff who is very glad the computer age is here. Kenn would not like to run his salon without a computer. His previous salon was totally computerized, and he hopes his new one will be soon. Computers help Kenn with the business side of hairdressing in scheduling appointments, doing the payroll, keeping an inventory of all retail sales in the shop, and handling all his bookkeeping chores. The computer is a true timesaver for Kenn. For example, instead of taking six to eight hours to do the payroll every week, the computer lets him finish this task in minutes and even prints out the payroll checks. But beyond this, the computer is an aid in the artistic side of hairdressing. By just pushing a few keys on the computer keyboard, Kenn can find out the correct hair color for individual clients as well as the date of their last permanent. With computer imaging, clients will soon know exactly what they will look like with a certain hairstyle and color. In the future, Kenn believes that clients will not have to wait until they arrive at a salon to get this visual image of themselves. Through direct computer linkups with salons, clients will be able to tell hairdressers what they want to look like for a special event even before they arrive for their appointments.

C is for Curator, Composer, and Copy Editor

COPY EDITOR   L.T. Brown is one of several copy editors at the *Indianapolis News*. Copy editors review and edit the work of reporters so it is ready to be set in type. At the start of L.T.'s day, thirty or forty stories may be stored in the newspaper's computer system waiting to be edited. Reporters have written the stories and given them to their editors who may have made some changes. The editors have also placed instructions on the stories detailing what kind of headlines are to be used and what the size of the story should be (column length and width). These stories are then sent to the copy chief—the editor who parcels out assignments and makes sure that the copy editors are working on what is needed. All this is done by computer on most newspapers.

L.T. pulls a story up on his computer monitor, and the copyediting process begins. As L.T. reads through the copy, he edits. At times, he must do considerable rewriting to meet space specifications that are sometimes so tight that he may substitute the word "try" for "attempt." By the press of a button on his computer, L.T. can tell whether the story is the correct length. When a story is the correct length, L.T. writes the headline and then sends it to the copy chief who glances through it for any errors L.T. has not caught and sends it to typesetting. The computer has truly replaced the copy editor's pencil.

D is for Detective, Designer, and Doctor

DOCTOR Bob Cravens is a doctor who believes that the computer is becoming an intrinsic part of medicine. At present, the main application of the computer for him, besides handling the business of running his office, is for doing research. Bob points out that a tremendous amount of medical data is available on CD-ROM, which makes it very easy for him to access journal articles and pictures. In fact research has become so easy that he is now able to find years and years of medical research on a topic in a matter of seconds. Bob also carries a portable computer in his pocket, which he uses to keep appointment information, phone numbers, and his calendar of activities and meetings. As an orthopedic surgeon, Bob is looking forward to the day when he is doing hip replacement surgery with the aid of the computer. At present, it is very costly to use the computer for this procedure. However, using the computer in hip replacement surgery allows for a prosthesis that exactly fits the patient's hip to be constructed during surgery rather than having to trim the bone to fit the prosthesis.

E is for Editor, Engineer, and Educator

EDUCATOR   Rita Daniels is a public school teacher who is enthusiastic about computers. Rita is part of the HOTS (higher order thinking skills) program, which is designed to teach children through the use of computers. In order to work with the HOTS program, she participated in a summer training program. This computer program puts children in a specific situation. In the first fifteen minutes of class, the children learn the logical way of thinking about a problem through a teacher-led discussion. Then the children begin working with computers to explore and find the answers to open-ended questions. The children also use the electronic encyclopedia, which has an appealing multimedia approach combining text, graphics, and sound. For example, the encyclopedia lets the children research President John F. Kennedy and actually hear important speeches in the president's own voice. It is not just her students who are using the computer. Rita uses the HyperCard program to create lessons for her students. She can select pictures and put them directly into their computer lesson along with her own voiced comments.

Children in this two-year computer program, which usually starts in the fourth grade, show greater gains than children in other Chapter I programs. Studies have shown that after third grade, repetition through drill and practice no longer motivates children. Not only does working with the computer motivate and stimulate students, other advantages to working with the computer include:

- reaching children with different learning styles
- helping children realize that no matter how many mistakes they make, the computer will wait for them to get it right before moving on
- forcing children to do correct work as the computer will not accept haphazard work
- improving children's hand-eye coordination skills
- permitting children to escape the embarrassment of turning in work with sloppy handwriting and poor spelling

The use of the computer is increasing each year in schools. In the not-too-distant future, all teachers will be using computers in their classrooms.

F is for Farmer, Food Inspector, and Fire Fighter

FIRE FIGHTER   David L. Klingler is the chief inspector of a fire prevention division. When he began working at the fire station in 1986, all files were manual and all reports were typewritten. David, who used his home computer for playing games, began taking the schedules home to put on his computer. The chief was so impressed with David's work that he purchased a computer for the firehouse. Admitting every mistake in the book before learning how to use the computer, David ultimately succeeded in giving the computer a vital role at his fire station.

Today, the fire alarm system is completely automated. The computer now gives the station ready access to information about all the buildings in the district. By pushing a few keys, David or any of the other fire fighters can find out the size of the building, the type of alarm system that the building has, and who occupies the building. The location of fire extinguishers also is stored on the computer as well as when they were last serviced. Furthermore, all the fire inspectors now carry hand-held computers instead of clipboards to inspection sites. They punch in record numbers and codes along with a 144-letter description to complete inspections. When the inspectors return to the station, the information can be uploaded quickly into the station's computer, and in less than one minute a printout of the inspection is available. The computer also has helped the fire fighters cut 95 percent of all the writing involved in keeping track of hoses and hydrants. In addition, the station can get information and reports on fire responses and fatalities by linking their computer to one in Washington, D.C. The computer has truly become a fire fighter at David's station.

G is for Geologist, Graphic Artist, and General Manager

GENERAL MANAGER   Mark Goff studied music and business in school and is now the general manager of a music store. At his store the employees cannot do their jobs without using the computer, as everything they do is linked to the computer. All sales transactions and product information is entered into the computer. A record of the store's inventory and sales is kept on the computer. Customer correspondence and inner-office memorandums are done on the computer. The computer even is used to produce the company's bar codes. Here's an example of how the store uses its computer system: Mark just purchased two trombones. They were immediately entered in the computer as a purchase. Then bar code labels were printed to identify the instruments. The repair shop input the work history of each instrument. This allows the music store to update an instrument's condition in the computer if it were to return to the store for resale or repair. Another task the computer has assumed is keeping track of the musical instruments the music store leases to over one hundred schools in the state. This involves billing over one thousand customers every month—a formidable job without the computer. Even though his store is completely computerized, Mark's background only includes one computer course, which was programming. He points out that most of the computer programs the store uses are very user-friendly. Because the menu program is so good, most staff members can usually figure out at once how to use the computer for their tasks.

H is for Historian, Hotel Staffer, and Horse Farm Owner

HORSE FARM OWNER   At Glenmore Farm in Lexington, Kentucky, the owners Barbara, Clay, and Jeff Camp are using computers to help them run their 285-acre horse farm. An amazing amount of data have been stored on the computer for each of the approximately 175 horses on the farm at any one time. With this information, the Camps are able to know the exact location on the farm of each horse and what kind of horse it is from a yearling to a racehorse. The computer also is used to keep track of breeding dates and when horses should foal. If anyone on the farm needs to have the health history of a horse, know when a horse needs a blacksmith, or when a horse will come in season, the answer is stored in the computer. Information about the arrival and departure of horses also can be found in the computer. Some mares from other states only visit the farm seasonally for breeding purposes. Information about what van company will be transporting a horse and what necessary health papers must go with it also can be found in the computer files.

When farm manager Jeff Camp goes on his daily visit to the barn, he does not bring pencil and paper but a laptop computer to note any actions he has taken with the horses. At the end of his daily rounds, he takes the laptop back to the office and uploads the data he has entered into the computer's master files. The computer operates throughout the day at Glenmore Farm. All the billing and check writing to pay bills and payroll are done on the computer. Besides instantly providing information about the horses, the computer saves the farm money. When it is time to take the year's records to the accountant, everything is already itemized. Barbara believes that if the computer were not helping them run the farm, they would need to hire additional people. She also finds the computer invaluable in researching the background of horses. By using a computer data bank such as Jockey Club, she can check a horse's parentage, age, track earnings, and sales results. She even can register a horse by using the computer modem.

I is for Instructor, Investigator, and Indexer

INDEXER   An index is the alphabetical list of names and subjects together with the page numbers that tell where they appear in the text of a book. Indexers compile these lists, which are typically found in the back of books. Claire Bolton feels very lucky to have the computer help her with her work as an indexer. There are special programs that she uses to do this work. The computer has freed her from worrying so much about clerical details and allowed her to concentrate on the quality of what she is producing. The advent of the computer has cut the number of indexers required on the staffs of book companies. Many indexers are freelancers, as is Claire.

J is for Judge, Jeweler, and Jailer

JAILER   Norman Bucker is assistant jail commander of a large metropolitan jail that houses 1,500 inmates. The computer system is up and running every day. It is a fantastic management tool, which lets Norman and others on the jail staff know myriad details about the prisoners just by pressing a few buttons. The computer has information on where prisoners are located, movement of prisoners, rule violations prisoners have committed, past stays in prison, prison escapes, and what type of prisoner an individual is. Information is so detailed that the staff is able to find every car that is registered to a prisoner's family.

At this large jail everything is done on the computer, from visitations to library visits for inmates to employee attendance records. The computer system makes it possible to send memos and contact individuals such as prosecutors without having to spend hours playing phone tag. Jail policy can be created, adjusted, or even changed without too much difficulty. Using the computer has helped the jail staff cut down on paperwork, is cost effective, and has improved the overall management of the jail.

K is for Kindergarten Teacher and Kennel Owner

KENNEL OWNER   Rick Smith is the owner of two kennels in Michigan. He realized that customers often made plans for the

care of their pets over the phone and then changed their instructions when the pets were left at the kennel. In order to keep the
pet owners happy and to provide the proper care for their pets,
Rick developed the software program KennelSoft. The program
is now being used by over three hundred different kennels
throughout the country. Rick points out that so much of the
successful operation of a kennel involves communication, and
the computer helps to eliminate problems by storing information
in such a way that everyone has access to it. For example, kennel
care givers need to know the proper diet for each animal, and the
computer stops workers from misreading another person's abbre-
viations or scribbles. The computer prints out a card that is put
on each pet's run. The card tells the animal's name, breed,
weight, color, and diet and lists any toys or other items that the
animal has brought to the kennel. (Rick has had animals come
with their own monogrammed Gucci luggage). By looking at the
computer printed card, an employee quickly can see what care
an animal requires and if the right animal is in a run.

Shawn Robertson, a manager at a kennel using KennelSoft,
says the computer is the heart of their business. Shawn explains
that every time a dog is checked in or out of the kennel, it is
entered in the computer data base. In addition, special notations
on personality problems can be stored in the computer. Shawn
adds that the computer also does their inventory and keeps track
of everything in the retail area. In addition, the computer is used
to determine how many animals can be accommodated at the
kennel. This is especially important during the busy holiday
periods, when so many different animals are vying for a limited
number of spaces.

The computer has been so helpful to Rick that he is able to
run his Michigan kennels in the winter from his home in Florida.
Every day by modem, Rick can find out how many different
animals entered and left his kennels and the number of animals
that were groomed. He is able to determine what the day's
income was as well as check on the inventory at each kennel.
The computer has enabled Rick to arrange his business so he can

have other people actually see to the day-to-day operations of his kennels.

Rick sees the computer as the catalyst for the development of chains of kennels. He believes that pet owners will get better care for their animals in these major operations because of the availability of professional advice on diet and animal health.

L is for Loan Officer, Legal Secretary, and Librarian

LIBRARIAN Suzanne Braun has been the librarian at the Indianapolis Zoo for the past five years. Suzanne, who has a master's degree in library science, points out that the computer classes are mandatory for librarians as the computer has become such an important tool in libraries. Like that of all librarians, much of her workday involves using the computer.

The Indianapolis Zoo is part of the Indiana Department of Education's computer access network (IDEANET), which ties together schools and businesses in the state of Indiana to provide information to students and teachers. Using a modem and this free computer system, Suzanne spent one hour recently with a third grade class. During this live computer chat, students took turns typing in their questions about animals and received immediate input from Suzanne on their computer. She also spends many hours a day doing research on the computer system that links all public, academic, and special libraries across the country. This system enables her to track down books and articles through interlibrary loan and have a copy of the book or article sent to her. Suzanne is also one of twelve zoo and aquarium librarians in the United States who share information. For example, when she has created a bibliography on a certain animal, the information can be downloaded onto a floppy and then sent and uploaded into another zoo librarian's system in another part of the country.

Suzanne spends additional time on the computer going through her e-mail messages and sending replies back to teachers and students wanting zoo related information. She also uses e-mail to communicate with other zoo librarians. She sorts through her e-mail and keeps the information that will be helpful to zoo staff members. Because Suzanne works at a small specialized library, she is using a filing system for disks that works best for the zoo. She has her floppy disks stored topically and indexed. Due to the large capacity of her hard drive, considerable information can be stored right in the computer's memory. Suzanne considers the computer a necessity in order to do her job as a librarian efficiently.

M is for Mathematician, Mechanic, and Music Copyist

MUSIC COPYIST   Music copyists transcribe each individual musical part from a score onto paper. For example, a copyist will go through a complete score and write out the entire part for the violin, making it much easier for the violinist to play his or her part. In the past, copying was done by hand with a special pen. Today, however, copyists can play on a keyboard directly into a computer. The information is then translated into printed notations.

Jeff Wiedenfeld and his wife, Julie, run Blue Note Engraving, a company that copies music. Their company is fully computerized, and the speed of the computer is very important in getting music to the clients on time. According to Jeff, the computer does it all. Publishing houses, music groups, and composers need copies quickly, and with the modem he can get copy to a publisher—even one in London—without much delay. Julie and Jeff do no copying by hand because they have instructed the computer to do it all. Although their business is based in the Midwest, they have clients throughout the country.

N is for Nurse, Nutritionist, and Newspaper Employee

Newspaper Employee   Karen Braeckel is the manager of the educational services department of a major metropolitan newspaper. Her basic job is to encourage the reading of newspapers in the classroom. The Newspaper in Education program develops educational materials for teachers to use with students and gives workshops on using the newspaper in the classroom. Most of the work is done on the community relations department's four computers. Karen writes articles on the computer and uses it to write memos to pass on to other newspaper employees. When one of the articles is ready to be printed in the newspaper, Karen sends it directly down to the composing room. Karen is a true computer buff who says she could not possibly produce what she does today if she did not have access to a computer.

Karen Sprunger also works in educational services. She had never used a computer until she began working at a smaller newspaper seven years ago. She learned how to use the computer by simple trial and error. In her present job, Karen uses the computer for a variety of tasks including: writing letters, editing or compiling materials for teachers, designing student worksheets, formatting reports for committees, and creating special calendars and materials. What she likes best about the computer is the freedom it gives her to move text. Karen spends her workdays creating pages exactly the way she wants them to look. Karen enjoys using the computer in her job and is happy that she no longer has to spend as much time cutting and pasting layouts.

O is for Optometrist and Officer in the Army

Officer in the Army   Dana Ball was issued a computer before her freshman year began at West Point, and when she graduated she took the computer with her to her first assignment. At West Point the computers were interfaced with Kermit—a network mail system that allowed cadets to log on to the system and communicate both with other cadets in the corps and with professors. She also was able to exchange information with any other school with e-mail and to transfer mail to the other academies. Dana used the computer for her classes from English to calculus. She also spent five to eight hours a day on it in her senior year, as she had selected the systems engineering track as her engineering area and all work was done on the computer.

Today, Dana is a second lieutenant and the executive officer for a two-to-four-hundred soldier advanced individual training company. Her main assignment is to relieve the administrative burden of her commander. She plans the training of the soldiers and uses the computer to create hard copy of the training schedule. In order to accomplish this mission, she spends time creating short-, medium-, and long-range calendars on the computer. Without the computer, it would take Dana countless hours to produce her weekly training schedule. By using the computer she is able to bring up previous schedules and keep all the items that remain the same each week such as wake-up and bed-check times. The computer is also an invaluable tool in handling her other duties. Dana uses the Harvard Graphics program to print awards for the soldiers. And she uses the computer to handle the paperwork for her other duties, which include serving as the local unit drug and alcohol testing officer, the moral welfare and recreation officer, and a member of the officer club council and the arts and crafts councils.

P is for Postal Clerk, Paralegal, and Pharmacist

PHARMACIST   Rosie Perez is a pharmacist at a large chain drugstore. Call in a refill or hand her a prescription for a refill, and she will quickly pull the prescription up on her computer. Then the computer will print the label. Rosie fills the prescription from the label. If you have a new prescription, she will enter it into the computer, which will then print the label. The first time customers visit her drug store to fill a prescription, they also complete a form giving information about allergies, health conditions, and prescription insurance plans. Rosie enters all of this information in the computer. If a customer's new prescription does not go with other medications or is contraindicated because of allergies or health conditions, the computer will alert Rosie to this fact. In addition, the computer will print insurance forms for customers needing them. It also will bill insurance companies directly for some customers. Besides serving as a pharmacist's helper and bookkeeper, the computer also keeps inventory of all the drugs that are sold and updates the inventory on a weekly basis. The inventory list goes by computer to company headquarters to that drugs can be automatically replenished when the weekly supply truck arrives. Rosie considers the computer to be a valuable aid in completing her work.

Q is for Quilter and Quality-Control Technician

QUALITY-CONTROL TECHNICIAN   Engineers design the printers manufactured by the Silicon Valley company where Mary Lai works as a quality-control technician. Her job is to make sure the production model meets the engineers' design standards. Before the advent of computerized testing, most quality-control work was done by selecting a sample of the factory's products and then measuring or testing the product to see if it worked as it was designed to. In some cases this actually involved tearing products apart to see that they were made correctly. Using this approach meant that not every product could be tested. In Mary's company every printer is tested to ensure it meets the design parameters. This is possible because the company uses a computer-based system with special sensors that quickly can tell if the printer is meeting acceptable limits. The computer is actually making 100 percent quality control possible.

R is for Realtor, Reporter, and Reservation Clerk

RESERVATION CLERK   Carol Love is a reservation sales representative for an international airline. During her eight-and-one-half hour workday, she spends approximately seven hours and forty minutes in front of a computer handling requests for reservations. She also can change or cancel reservations simply by modifying the record on the computer. Carol has to knowledgeable about her company's policies and procedures as well as be aware of special promotions. When Carol first went to work for the airline in 1968, all her work was done by slides. Computers were introduced in 1969 and since then have been upgraded frequently to more efficient models that have much less downtime. Even though the computer makes Carol's job much easier, she still finds herself, at times, suffering from eyestrain at the end of her shift, even with special screens designed to reduce glare.

S is for Secretary, Sheriff, and Systems Accountant

SYSTEMS ACCOUNTANT   Les Gisler works on a computer four or five hours a day as a systems accountant. He uses his terminal to interact with the mainframe to extract financial reports for end users who are usually staff accountants. He also uses the computer to solve accounting problems and improve the handling of information. Away from the computer, he trains accountant technicians in the use of hardware as well as the programs that he has designed. Les also has the task of coordinating major system changes between the programming staff and the accounting function.

The position of systems accountant requires a solid background in both computer science and accounting. Les was introduced to computers in the early 1970s, when he was in the army and took a data systems course that covered programming and included an introduction to hardware and systems analysis. After he left the service, Les completed his degree in accounting. Several years later his growing interest in the data processing side of accounting compelled him to return to school to earn an associate's degree in computer technology. This additional degree helped him obtain his present position as a systems accountant.

T is for Therapist, Ticket Seller, and Tennis Coach

Tennis Coach   P.A. Nilhagen is a tennis coach of professional and college players as well as junior players. During a match a tennis expert can key into a computer what is happening on the court. The computer can then produce charts giving coaches and players a statistical breakdown on such things as percentage of good first serves, the effectiveness of a player's serve in the deuce vs advantage court, a player's rate of success in going to the net, and the number of unforced errors committed. P.A. has used the computer with ATP tour player Todd Witsken and with several professional and college players. He finds that the computer-generated information about a match provides significant help, especially when he is unable to attend a player's match. P.A. also has discovered that most players are not pleased to read the printout of their match and see the specific classification of their errors. According to P.A., what the computer cannot produce is a chart of the player's mental state during the match, which is critical in understanding when and why players make errors.

The computer is not just used in tennis to chart play during matches. P.A. considers it a very helpful tool in making draws for tournaments. For example, if a tournament is being held with a draw of sixty-four players, the draw would take hours to make on paper. With the computer the time can be reduced to eight seconds, once the necessary information has been keyed in. P.A. also finds using the computer at tournament check-in desks to be very helpful, especially in determining if players have current USTA (United States Tennis Association) numbers.

U is for Underwriter, Urban Planner, and Undergraduate

UNDERGRADUATE   Before most college students enter the job market, they have started working with computers. Besides having science laboratories, colleges now have computer laboratories. And many colleges have elaborate networks that connect to every living group or even every student's room. Aaron Ball is a senior at a private university with a double major in Spanish and political science. Similar to most undergraduates, he took a computer class in high school and has taken two classes in college. Aaron has his own computer at college, and he also uses the computers on campus. He believes that word processing is critical to his academic success, since college professors expect all assignments to be word processed. He keeps all his work on disks so that revisions can be made easily. And he also uses the computer in managing his time as he keeps a running file on his current projects. In addition, as president of the university Political Science Association, he uses graphics programs extensively to print schedules and announcements of upcoming events and speakers. After graduation Aaron plans to enter law school, and his computer will be going right along with him.

V is for Veterinarian and Volunteer

VOLUNTEER   Volunteering has always been a part of the American culture and one of its greatest resources. In recent years the number of volunteers has swelled, and many of these volunteers are computer buffs who are using the computer in their volunteer work. George Kratz is a volunteer who serves as the director of a bridge club. Since bridge involves considerable scoring, George uses the computer to handle these calculations smoothly and efficiently. Furthermore, he can have the scores available almost as soon as a playing session is over. Bridge players, especially duplicate players, are very competitive and are very eager to know their scores. Most avid bridge players use their scores to accumulate master points. When they have sufficient points, they will become life masters—a title recognizing their expertise. The computer is used to keep track of these points for club members. The club's mailing list is stored on the computer so information can be sent quickly to members. The monthly schedule of games also is done on the computer. The speed of the computer helps George run the club games efficiently and keep the players happy.

W is for Writer, Ward Attendant, and Weather Forecaster

WEATHER FORECASTER   In 1982, Chuck Lofton became a full-time weather forecaster for a national television network and started spending most of his workday on the computer. He creates his own graphics for his weather segments on television; however, he also can get computer-generated graphics. Chuck accesses all his weather information via the computer from the national weather station. He can even get an update on the weather immediately before he goes on the air.

Chuck believes that advances in technology will bring higher resolution and cleaner pictures, more animation, and better presentations of the weather on television. At present, RADAR NEXAR (next generation radar sites) are being built throughout the United States. RADAR NEXAR will allow weather forecasters to analyze a storm in sixteen different ways. Weather forecasters literally will be able to see inside a storm, find out how high the winds are, and determine how much rain the storm will produce. This will be especially helpful when the weather forecaster is tracking severe weather. Using a computer is an absolute necessity for weather forecasters as it helps them forecast the weather more accurately.

X is for X-ray Technologist

X-RAY TECHNOLOGIST   Constance Murray works in the x-ray department of a major metropolitan hospital. She points out that the application of computer technology has absolutely revolutionized the field of radiology. Computed tomographic (CT) scanning has employed computers since its inception. In CT scanning three-dimensional reconstruction of two-dimensional images is possible with computers. These three-dimensional anatomic images can be rotated to visualize the structure in any plane. Orbital fractures and many facial reconstructive surgeries utilize these modalities. Computer technology also is employed in digital radiography and fluoroscopy, which are becoming routine procedures in the clinical setting. Magnetic resonance imaging (MRI) also applies computer technology similar to CT. With MRI, images of patient anatomy are stored in the computer as bits of data, which can then be printed on film for hard copy and storage retrieval. Anatomical images digitized on a computer also allow manipulation of the image to highlight pathology or better demonstrate organs not otherwise seen well. According to Constance, the advances the computer has brought to radiology make her believe that "Star Trek"–quality medical care is not far away.

Y is for YMCA Employee

YMCA EMPLOYEE   William Graham works as vice-president/controller at YMCA headquarters in a midwestern city. The main computer is at headquarters and is linked to computers at the other YMCAs in the eight county area. There also are several PCs in the headquarters' office and in branches that help with correspondence, creating brochures, and monitoring program attendance. William says that the computer really helps him to do his job, as nonprofit organizations have to collect so much data for reports to the United Way and various units of government. The computer is used to keep track of revenues for the monthly reports and all financial work in the accounting and payroll departments. It also is used to keep track of all the members and the programs in which they participate.

Z is for Zoologist and Zoo Manager

ZOO MANAGER   F. Kevin Gaza works in the business management office of the zoo. He says that the computer helps the zoo in business applications, animal management, and animal record keeping. ARKS is the data base system used in keeping a detailed history of all animals. This is very important as it helps to avoid the interbreeding of vanishing wildlife. For example, there are not a lot of Siberian tigers in captivity, so finding a mate is not easy. However, by using the ARKS data base, the zookeeper can find every Siberian tiger in captivity and know what its gene makeup is. ISIS (International Species Information System) keeps such detailed information on its data base that the exact breeding time of any animal can be swiftly ascertained for stud purposes.

CHAPTER TEN

Exploring Future Computer Careers

T he *Time* magazine Man of the Year in 1982 (the computer) will continue to make waves in the job market in the twenty-first century. Although the explosive growth of the computer industry has slowed down, it is still growing faster than most large industries. Some areas within the industry will explode and grow at absolutely fantastic rates in the future. What the next hot job areas will be depends on emerging technology and applications. Computer buffs need constantly to stay abreast of what is happening in the computer industry to find promising career opportunities. For example, the quality of computer graphics improved immeasurably with the development of the laser printer. This spawned the creation of the desktop publishing industry, when the price of laser printers and desktop computers dropped dramatically.

Here is a list of job areas that computer buffs may wish to explore in the future as many industry experts see promising career opportunities in these areas:

COMMUNICATIONS   Organizations will continue to link computers together in local- and wide-area networks so the users can share peripherals and files and exchange information. Computer professionals will be needed to design and implement these systems. Fiber optics will bring sweeping changes in communications. Engineers with knowledge of fiber optics are needed.

SYSTEMS INTEGRATION   Organizations want to integrate different hardware, operating systems, and applications software so that they can share information with each other. As so many organizations have this need, both in-house staff and outside consultants are needed as system integrators.

SECURITY   Because the reliable operation of computers is so essential to organizations, the need for staff in the area of security is growing. Organizations do not want their computers to be infected with viruses or have their operation disrupted because the equipment is damaged or destroyed. Security specialists prevent access to the computer system by unauthorized people, set up plans to handle disasters, maintain back-up copies of important information, and audit the security of the system. They work in-house or as consultants to organizations.

CASE TOOLS   Computer-Aided Software Engineering (CASE) tools automate many aspects of software design making it easier and faster for programmers to create new programs and revise existing ones. Computer professionals are needed to develop new CASE tools as organizations increasingly use these tools to create their own software.

MULTIMEDIA   Interest is steadily increasing in this computer-based method of presenting materials that combine text, sound, and graphics and emphasize interactivity. A CD-ROM drive provides the storage capacity needed to handle the graphics and sound. Both hardware and software experts will be needed to make multimedia truly commercial.

EXPERT SYSTEMS   These systems are computer programs that contain much of the knowledge an expert in a specific field would use to make a decision. Such systems are being used by doctors to suggest diagnoses. Organizations, especially businesses, are actively seeking professionals, called knowledge engineers, who have the skills to design and develop expert systems.

Computer Careers in Other Job Areas

In the future, computer buffs can look forward to finding computers practically everywhere. No matter where you seek a job, a computer is likely to be involved in some way in your performance of that job. Your home life also will be greatly changed by what your home computer can do for you. Technological innovations in the use of computers have only begun to scratch the surface of their potential. Some researchers believe that the advances will be so great that it is very difficult to make predictions of how the computer will be used just twenty years from now.

Changes Are Coming

In the twenty-first century, you may find computers being used in some of the following ways, according to the computer buffs interviewed in this book. And you as a computer buff may be involved in making these things happen through your job working with computers.

1. Can you imagine home computers running robots? No longer will busy people have to waste their time looking for someone to come in and do their household chores. The robots will be cooking, cleaning, doing the wash, and even cutting the grass thanks to the technology that will be able to interface home computers to robots. To make it even more fantastic, your robot can be programmed to have the personality of Julia Roberts or Tom Cruise.

2. Have you ever been flustered by not being able to find your car keys? Have you ever run out of gas on the freeway? Your troubles will soon be over because computerized cars will be in the marketplace. In fact, some of the features that tomorrow's computerized cars will have are already in today's cars. On-board computers are able to figure how many miles worth of fuel remain in the tank and estimate arrival times for long trips. However, these features are only the beginning. In the future, you will be able to throw away your keys because the coded touchpads on the doors and dashboard will allow you to open the door and start the car. Rear television monitors will replace your car's outside mirrors. You will be able to avoid hitting objects such as dogs, children, bikes, and other cars thanks to a sonar detection system. Forget about stopping at the gas station to buy a map; your car will always know where it is on its own video map and even know the distance to your destination. At the present time, it looks like you will still be doing the driving, but who really knows what the future will bring!

3. Because of 3-D interaction you will be able to have any kind of world your heart desires. You will have reached utopia thanks to computer technology. By just going down the street to the virtual-reality store, you will be able to enjoy coffee in a cafe in Paris or be cruising down the Rhine in Germany. You will be able to visit a zoo and be in the cage with the gorillas or swim in the water with the dolphins.

4. Leading the way into the next generation of computers is something termed artificial intelligence (AI). It is fascinating to think that computers will be able to imitate human intelligence at levels including thinking, common sense, self-teaching, and even decision making. Even now, AI is being used in expert systems to help doctors pinpoint what disease a patient may have. Artificial intelligence also will make it possible for you to ask your computer a question and get an answer. This is even beginning now with information retrieval from data bases.

5. Voice recognition, which today is still in its infancy, will be able to handle a larger vocabulary, different voices, and

continuous speech. Today, based on research in voice recognition, the National Security Agency is able to monitor overseas telephone calls. It is hoped that elderly people and the handicapped soon will be able to use a typewriterlike machine with a large spoken vocabulary so they can communicate better with others.

6. Fast food today will be even faster tomorrow when a multi-armed robot is fixing and filling orders, collecting money, giving change, sweeping the floor, and even clearing tables. You may think that this only happens on television shows, but you are wrong. The robot even will be able to detect overcooked hamburgers and toss them in the trash. Furthermore, it will be able to go anywhere in the restaurant while its independently operating arms will be efficiently performing different tasks. And only one human engineer will be needed per shift to keep it running!

7. What a union! Computer technology will combine with telephone systems to create hybrid phones. These will not be ordinary phones. You not only will be able to send and retrieve your messages, you will use the phone to teach yourself a foreign language, and the phone will even remind you when it is time to send your relatives' birthday cards. You might be getting your wake-up calls from a computer that even will be able to turn on lights, air conditioners, and the vacuum cleaner. The telephone of the twenty-first century will use fiber optics, laser, and satellite technology.

8. The computer in the future will help handicapped individuals who have no physical movement. This will be done through brain waves. For example, letters will be flashed on a screen, and as soon as a letter is recognized brain waves will change.

9. Computers will make prosthetic devices more realistically. These artificial devices even will be able to perform small motor skills. Computers will also control artificial organs. Parts of tomorrow's computers will not just be mechanical like today's computers; they will have smaller parts that will be chemically and biologically controlled motors.

10. In your lifetime, the daily paper as you know it may no longer exist. People will have everything on CD-ROM and hardly ever look at hard copy. Today's CD-ROM will be reduced to the size of a slide, be read by laser, and hold several times more than does the current CD-ROM. Computers will be part of the home entertainment center. Your television and computer will be combined.

Preparing for Your Future Career

Read as much as you can about the computer industry to find out where the jobs are and what the latest technology is. Explore the field by working part-time and in the summer or by participating in an internship or a cooperative education program. Employees value practical work experience. If you will be getting a degree in computer science, you can be certain the program is a quality one if it is certified by the Accreditation Board for Engineering and Technology, Inc. (ABET), or the Computing Sciences Accreditation Board, Inc. (CSAB). A list of these schools can be found in appendix A.

Remember, too, that computer buffs can find satisfying careers in government, business, education, manufacturing, and anywhere computers are being used. If you will be going into business, be sure to get a well-rounded education. According to Max Messmer, chairman of Accountemps, while specialized skills are in growing demand in today's workplace, a general awareness of a broad range of disciplines will allow workers to better apply those skills within a company.

Accredited Programs in Computing

T he following list is of accredited computer science and computer engineering programs. The year of accreditation appears by the university name and degree. The list is reprinted with permission from the Computer Science Accreditation Commission (CSAC) of the Computing Sciences Accreditation Board (CSAB) and by the Engineering Accreditation Commission (EAC) of the Accreditation Board of Engineering and Technology (ABET).

ALABAMA

AUBURN UNIVERSITY
B.S. Computer Science**   1987
B.S. Computer Engineering (with or without   1987
Cooperative Education)*

UNIVERSITY OF ALABAMA
B.S. Computer Science in the College of   1990
Engineering and College of Arts and Science**

UNIVERSITY OF ALABAMA IN HUNTSVILLE
B.S. Computer Science**   1988

B.S. Computer Engineering (with or without
Cooperative Education)*   1992

UNIVERSITY OF SOUTH ALABAMA
B.S. Computer and Information Science,   1988
Computer Science Specialization**

ALASKA

UNIVERSITY OF ALASKA FAIRBANKS
B.S. Computer Science**   1991

ARIZONA

ARIZONA STATE UNIVERSITY
B.S.E. Computer Systems Engineering*   1980
B.S. Computer Science**   1992

NORTHERN ARIZONA UNIVERSITY
B.S. Computer Science and Engineering*   1984

UNIVERSITY OF ARIZONA
B.S. Computer Engineering*   1987

ARKANSAS

UNIVERSITY OF ARKANSAS AT FAYETTEVILLE
B.S. Computer Systems Engineering*   1991

UNIVERSITY OF ARKANSAS AT LITTLE ROCK
B.S. Computer Science**   1990

CALIFORNIA

CALIFORNIA POLYTECHNIC STATE UNIVERSITY,
SAN LUIS OBISPO
B.S. Computer Science**   1986

CALIFORNIA STATE UNIVERSITY, CHICO
B. S. Computer Science,   1987
General, Math/Science, and Systems Options**
B.S. Computer Engineering*   1989

CALIFORNIA STATE UNIVERSITY, FULLERTON
B.S. Computer Science**   1988

CALIFORNIA STATE UNIVERSITY, LONG BEACH
B.S. Computer Science and Engineering*   1974

CALIFORNIA STATE UNIVERSITY, NORTHRIDGE
B.S. Computer Science**   1987

CALIFORNIA STATE UNIVERSITY, SACRAMENTO
B.S. Computer Science**   1986
B.S. Computer Engineering*   1989

CALIFORNIA STATE UNIVERSITY, SAN BERNARDINO
B.S. Computer Science**   1990

CALIFORNIA STATE UNIVERSITY, STANISLAUS
B.S. Computer Science**   1986

SAN JOSE STATE UNIVERSITY
B.S. Computer Engineering*   1991

SANTA CLARA UNIVERSITY
B.S. Computer Engineering*   1987

UNIVERSITY OF CALIFORNIA, BERKELEY
B.S. Computer Science*   1983

UNIVERSITY OF CALIFORNIA, DAVIS
B.S. Computer Science and Engineering*   1989

UNIVERSITY OF CALIFORNIA, LOS ANGELES
B.S. Computer Science and Engineering*   1986

UNIVERSITY OF CALIFORNIA, SANTA BARBARA
B.A. Computer Science**   1986
B.S. Computer Science**   1986

UNIVERSITY OF CALIFORNIA, SANTA CRUZ
B.S. Computer Engineering*   1989

UNIVERSITY OF CALIFORNIA,
SAN FRANCISCO
B.S. Computer Science**   1987

UNIVERSITY OF SOUTHERN CALIFORNIA
B.S. Computer Science**   1988

UNIVERSITY OF THE PACIFIC
B.S. Computer Science**   1990
B.S. Computer Engineering (with or without   1983
Cooperative Education)*

COLORADO

UNITED STATES AIR FORCE ACADEMY
B.S. Computer Science**   1986

UNIVERSITY OF COLORADO, BOULDER
B.S. Electrical and Computer Engineering*   1982

UNIVERSITY OF COLORADO, COLORADO SPRINGS
B.S. Computer Science**   1989

CONNECTICUT

CENTRAL CONNECTICUT STATE UNIVERSITY
B.S. Computer Science**   1990

UNIVERSITY OF BRIDGEPORT
B.S. Computer Engineering (with or without   1989
Cooperative Education)*

UNIVERSITY OF CONNECTICUT
B.S. Computer Science and Engineering*   1972

SOUTHERN CONNECTICUT STATE UNIVERSITY
B.S. Computer Science**   1992

DISTRICT OF COLUMBIA

AMERICAN UNIVERSITY
B.S. Computer Science**   1987

GEORGE WASHINGTON UNIVERSITY
B.S. Computer Science**	1987
B.S. Computer Engineering*	1984

HOWARD UNIVERSITY
B.S. Systems and Computer Science**	1988

FLORIDA

FLORIDA ATLANTIC UNIVERSITY
B.S. Computer Science**	1991

FLORIDA INSTITUTE OF TECHNOLOGY
B.S. Computer Engineering*	1983

FLORIDA STATE UNIVERSITY
B.S. Computer and Information Sciences**	1987

UNIVERSITY OF CENTRAL FLORIDA
B.S. Computer Science**	1989
B.S. Computer Engineering*	1974

UNIVERSITY OF FLORIDA
B.S. Computer and Information Engineering Sciences (with or without Cooperative Education)*	1983

UNIVERSITY OF MIAMI
B.S. Computer Engineering*	1988

UNIVERSITY OF NORTH FLORIDA
B.S. Computer and Information Science, Computer Science Specialization**	1987

UNIVERSITY OF SOUTH FLORIDA
B.S. Computer Science**	1989
B.S. Computer Engineering*	1984

GEORGIA

ARMSTRONG STATE COLLEGE
B.S. Computer Science**	1991

GEORGIA INSTITUTE OF TECHNOLOGY

B.S. Information and Computer Science**	1986
B.S. Computer Engineering (with or without Cooperative Education)*	1991

ILLINOIS

UNIVERSITY OF ILLINOIS, CHICAGO

B.S. Computer Engineering*	1976

UNIVERSITY OF ILLINOIS, URBANA-CHAMPAIGN

B.S. Computer Engineering (with or without Cooperative Education)*	1978

INDIANA

BALL STATE UNIVERSITY

B.S./B.A. Computer Science (with or without Cooperative Education)**	1987

PURDUE UNIVERSITY

B.S. Computer Electrical Engineering (with or without Cooperative Education)*	1984

VALPARAISO UNIVERSITY

B.S. Computer Engineering (with or without Cooperative Education)*	1990

IOWA

IOWA STATE UNIVERSITY

B.S. Computer Science**	1986
B.S. Computer Engineering (with or without Cooperative Education)*	1979

KANSAS

KANSAS STATE UNIVERSITY

B.S. Computer Engineering*	1991
B.S. Computer Science**	1992

UNIVERSITY OF KANSAS
B.S. Computer Engineering*   1992

KENTUCKY

EASTERN KENTUCKY UNIVERSITY
B.S. Computer Science**   1991

LOUISIANA

LOUISIANA STATE UNIVERSITY IN BATON ROUGE
B.S. Computer Engineering*   1989

LOUISIANA STATE UNIVERSITY IN SHREVEPORT
B.S. Computer Science**   1991

LOUISIANA TECH UNIVERSITY
B.S. Computer Science**   1988

NORTHEAST LOUISIANA UNIVERSITY
B.S. Computer Science**   1987

SOUTHERN UNIVERSITY
B.S. Computer Science,   1989
Scientific Option**

TULANE UNIVERSITY
B.S. Computer Science**   1990

UNIVERSITY OF NEW ORLEANS
B.S. Computer Science**   1987

UNIVERSITY OF SOUTHWESTERN LOUISIANA
B.S. Computer Science**   1987

MARYLAND

LOYOLA COLLEGE IN MARYLAND
B.S. Computer Science**   1990

UNITED STATES NAVAL ACADEMY
B.S. Computer Science**   1987

MASSACHUSETTS

BOSTON UNIVERSITY
B.S. Computer Engineering*　　　　　　　　1983

MASSACHUSETTS INSTITUTE OF TECHNOLOGY
B.S. Computer Science and Engineering (with or　1978
without Cooperative Education)*

MERRIMACK COLLEGE
B.S. Electrical/Computer Engineering (with or　1966
without Cooperative Education)*

NORTHEASTERN UNIVERSITY
B.S. Computer Science**　　　　　　　　　1986

TUFTS UNIVERSITY
B.S. Computer Engineering Option in　　　　1982
Electrical Engineering*

UNIVERSITY OF MASSACHUSETTS AMHERST
B.S. Computer Systems Engineering*　　　　1978

UNIVERSITY OF MASSACHUSETTS DARTMOUTH
B.S. Computer Science*　　　　　　　　　1988
B.S. Computer Engineering*　　　　　　　1984

UNIVERSITY OF MASSACHUSETTS LOWELL
B.S. Computer Science**　　　　　　　　　1990

WORCESTER POLYTECHNIC INSTITUTE
B.S. Computer Science**　　　　　　　　　1986

MICHIGAN

OAKLAND UNIVERSITY
B.S. Computer Science**　　　　　　　　　1988
B.S. Computer Engineering (with or without　1979
Cooperative Education)*

UNIVERSITY OF MICHIGAN
B.S. Computer Engineering*　　　　　　　1976

WESTERN MICHIGAN UNIVERSITY
B.S. Computer Science,   1986
Theory and Analysis Option**
B.S. Computer Systems Engineering*   1985

MINNESOTA

ST. CLOUD STATE UNIVERSITY
B.S. Computer Science**   1989

UNIVERSITY OF MINNESOTA, DULUTH
B.S. Computer Science**   1989
B.S. Computer Engineering*   1989

MISSISSIPPI

JACKSON STATE UNIVERSITY
B.S. Computer Science,   1991
Mathematics-Oriented Concentration**

MISSISSIPPI STATE UNIVERSITY
B.S. Computer Science**   1986
B.S. Computer Engineering (with or without   1988
Cooperative Education)*

UNIVERSITY OF MISSISSIPPI
B.S. Computer Science**   1990

UNIVERSITY OF SOUTHERN MISSISSIPPI
B.S. Computer Science**   1987

MISSOURI

SOUTHWEST MISSOURI STATE UNIVERSITY
B.S. Computer Science**   1989

UNIVERSITY OF MISSOURI, COLUMBIA
B.S. Computer Engineering*   1983

UNIVERSITY OF MISSOURI, ROLLA
B.S. Computer Science**   1986

WASHINGTON UNIVERSITY
B.S. Computer Science and Engineering (with or   1977
without Cooperative Education)*

NEW HAMPSHIRE

UNIVERSITY OF NEW HAMPSHIRE
B.S. Computer Science**   1987

NEW JERSEY

FAIRLEIGH DICKINSON UNIVERSITY
B.S. Computer Science**   1987

NEW JERSEY INSTITUTE OF TECHNOLOGY
B.S. Computer Science**   1986

STEVENS INSTITUTE OF TECHNOLOGY
B.S. Computer Science**   1986
B.S. Computer Engineering*   1986

NEW MEXICO

NEW MEXICO STATE UNIVERSITY
B.S. Computer Science**   1988

UNIVERSITY OF NEW MEXICO
B.S. Computer Science**   1988
B.S. Computer Engineering*   1978

NEW YORK

CANISIUS COLLEGE
B.S. Computer Science**   1987

CLARKSON UNIVERSITY
B.S. Computer Engineering*   1991

CITY COLLEGE, CUNY
B.S. Computer Science**   1992

COLLEGE OF STATEN ISLAND, CUNY
B.S. Computer Science**   1989

PACE UNIVERSITY
B.S. Computer Science**   1986

POLYTECHNIC UNIVERSITY
B.S. Computer Science**   1988
B.S. Computer Engineering*   1991
(BROOKLYN AND FARMINGDALE CAMPUSES,
with or without Cooperative Education)

RENSSELAER POLYTECHNIC INSTITUTE
B.S. Computer and Systems Engineering (with   1978
or without Cooperative Education)*

ROCHESTER INSTITUTE OF TECHNOLOGY
B.S. Computer Science**   1989
B.S. Computer Engineering (Cooperative
Education)*   1987

STATE UNIVERSITY OF NEW YORK AT ALBANY
B.S. Computer Science**   1987

STATE UNIVERSITY OF NEW YORK AT
BINGHAMTON
B.S. Computer Science**   1989

STATE UNIVERSITY OF NEW YORK AT NEW PALTZ
B.S. Computer Science**   1991

STATE UNIVERSITY OF NEW YORK AT
STONY BROOK
B.S. Computer Engineering (option in   1991
Electrical Engineering)*

SYRACUSE UNIVERSITY
B.S. Computer Engineering*   1973

NORTH CAROLINA

APPALACHIAN STATE UNIVERSITY
B.S. Computer Science**   1988

NORTH CAROLINA STATE UNIVERSITY

B.S. Computer Science**	1987
B.S. Computer Engineering (with or without Cooperative Education)*	1990

NORTH DAKOTA

NORTH DAKOTA STATE UNIVERSITY

B.S. Computer Science**	1986

UNIVERSITY OF NORTH DAKOTA

B.A./B.S. Computer Science**	1987

OHIO

CASE WESTERN RESERVE UNIVERSITY

B.S. Computer Engineering (with or without Cooperative Education)*	1971

UNIVERSITY OF CINCINNATI

B.S. Computer Engineering (Cooperative Education)*	1987

UNIVERSITY OF DAYTON

B.S. Computer Science**	1991

UNIVERSITY OF TOLEDO

B.S. Computer Science and Engineering**	1991

WRIGHT STATE UNIVERSITY

B.S. Computer Science**	1987
B.S. Computer Engineering*	1984

OKLAHOMA

UNIVERSITY OF TULSA

B.S. Computer Science in the College of Arts and Science and the College of Engineering and Applied Science**	1988

OREGON

OREGON STATE UNIVERSITY
  B.S. Computer Engineering*   1985

PENNSYLVANIA

BUCKNELL UNIVERSITY
  B.S. Computer Science**   1991

CARNEGIE-MELLON UNIVERSITY
  B.S. Computer Engineering*   1989

DREXEL UNIVERSITY
  B.S. Computer Science**   1986

LEHIGH UNIVERSITY
  B.S. Computer Science in the   1987
  College of Engineering & Applied Science**
  B.S. Computer Engineering*   1987

PENNSYLVANIA STATE UNIVERSITY
  B.S. Computer Engineering (with or without   1991
  Cooperative Education)*

UNIVERSITY OF SCRANTON
  B.S. Computer Science**   1990

VILLANOVA UNIVERSITY
  B.S. Computer Science in the   1991
  College of Liberal Arts and Sciences**

RHODE ISLAND

UNIVERSITY OF RHODE ISLAND
  B.S. Computer Engineering*   1992

SOUTH CAROLINA

CLEMSON UNIVERSITY
  B.S. Computer Science**   1986

B.S. Computer Engineering (with or without   1988
Cooperative Education)*

COLLEGE OF CHARLESTON
B.S. Computer Science**   1992

UNIVERSITY OF SOUTH CAROLINA
B.S. Computer Science**   1990

WINTHROP UNIVERSITY
B.S. Computer Science**   1990

TEXAS

BAYLOR UNIVERSITY
B.S. Computer Science**   1987

PRAIRIE VIEW A&M UNIVERSITY
B.S. Computer Science**   1992

SOUTHERN METHODIST UNIVERSITY
B.S. Computer Engineering (with or without   1985
Cooperative Education)*

TEXAS CHRISTIAN UNIVERSITY
B.S. Computer Science**   1990

UNIVERSITY OF HOUSTON
B.S. Computer Science**   1987

UNIVERSITY OF NORTH TEXAS
B.S. Computer Science**   1986

UNIVERSITY OF TEXAS AT ARLINGTON
B.S. Computer Science and Engineering*   1983

UNIVERSITY OF TEXAS AT AUSTIN
B.S. Computer Engineering*   1988

UNIVERSITY OF TEXAS AT EL PASO
B.S. Computer Science**   1986

UTAH

BRIGHAM YOUNG UNIVERSITY
B.S. Computer Science**   1989

VIRGINIA

HAMPTON UNIVERSITY
B.S. Computer Science**   1989

NORFOLK STATE UNIVERSITY
B.S. Computer Science**   1991

OLD DOMINION UNIVERSITY
B.S. Computer Science**   1990
B.S. Computer Engineering (with or without   1989
Cooperative Education)*

RADFORD UNIVERSITY
B.S. Computer Science**   1992

VIRGINIA COMMONWEALTH UNIVERSITY
B.S. Computer Science**   1988

VIRGINIA POLYTECHNIC INSTITUTE AND
STATE UNIVERSITY
B.S. Computer Science*   1990

WASHINGTON

EASTERN WASHINGTON UNIVERSITY
B.S. Computer Science**   1987

PACIFIC LUTHERAN UNIVERSITY
B.S. Computer Science**   1989

UNIVERSITY OF WASHINGTON
B.S. Computer Engineering*   1988

WESTERN WASHINGTON UNIVERSITY
B.S. Computer Science**   1987

WEST VIRGINIA

WEST VIRGINIA UNIVERSITY
B.S. Computer Engineering*　　　　　　　　　1992

WISCONSIN

MILWAUKEE SCHOOL OF ENGINEERING
B.S. Computer Engineering*　　　　　　　　　1988

*Program is accredited by the Engineering Accreditation Commission of the Accreditation Board for Engineering and Technology.

**Program is accredited by the Computer Science Accreditation Commission of the Computing Sciences Accreditation Board.

***Program is dually accredited by the Engineering Accreditation Commission of the Accreditation Board for Engineering and Technology and the Computer Science Accreditation Commission of the Computing Sciences Accreditation Board.

APPENDIX B

Computer Industry-Related Organizations

The following list is of computer industry-related organizations. You can learn more about the computer industry by contacting these organizations. The organizations are listed alphabetically by name and include address, phone, and a brief description. Excerpted with permission from *Computer Industry Almanac*. Copyright © 1992, Computer Industry Almanac, Inc., 225 Allen Way, Incline Village, Nevada 89451–9608.

ABCD: The Microcomputer Industry Association, Inc.
450 East 22nd Street, Suite 230
Lombard, IL 60173
708–240–1818
Promotes and encourages professionalism and business ethics in the microcomputer industry.

ACM SIG Organizations
15 Broadway
New York, NY 10036
212–626–0611

ACM SIG on Architecture of Computer Systems
Design and organization of computer systems.

ACM SIG on Artificial Intelligence
Special-interest group on knowledge-based systems.

ACM SIG on Computer Graphics
Computer graphics R&D, technologies and applications.

ACM SIG on Computer Science Education
Development, implementation and evaluation of computer science programs and courses.

ACM SIG on Computer Uses in Education
Improved concepts, methods and policies for instructional computing.

ACM SIG on Design Automation
Computer applications in all phases of electrical and electronics design fields.

ACM SIG on Programming Languages
Practical and theoretical aspects on all programming languages.

American Association for Artificial Intelligence
445 Burgess Dr.
Menlo Park, CA 94025
415-328-3213
Scientific society for the study and application of artificial intelligence science and technology.

American Society for Information Science
8720 Georgia Ave., Ste. 501
Silver Spring, MD 20910
301-495-0900
Improve access to information through policy, technology, and research.

Association for Systems Management
1433 W. Bagley Rd., P.O. Box 38370
Cleveland, OH 44138–0370
216–243–6900
Continuing education to increase the competence of
information systems professionals.

Association for Women in Science
1522 K St., Ste. 820
Washington, DC 20005
202–408–0742
Expanding educational and career opportunities for women in
the sciences.

Computer Learning Foundation
P.O. Box 60007
Palo Alto, CA 94306–0007
FAX: 415–327–3349
Increase effective and ethical use of technology among
educators, parents, and youth.

Computer Musician Coalition
1024 W. Wilcox Ave.
Peoria, IL 61604
309–685–4843
Provides computer/music enthusiasts with service,
information, and products.

Data Processing Management Association
505 Busse Highway
Park Ridge, IL 60068
708–825–8124
Provides a broader understanding of the methods and
principles of data processing software, hardware, and
management techniques.

The EDP Auditors Association, Inc.
3701 Algonquin Rd., Ste. 1010
Rolling Meadows, IL 60008
708–253–1545
Advancement of EDP audit and control community through
education, research, and professional programs.

IEEE Computer Society
1730 Massachusetts Ave. NW
Washington, DC 20036
202–371–0101
Serves professionals in all aspects of computing. Promotes
technical interaction in a variety of programs and activities.

Institute of Electrical and Electronics Engineers, Inc.
345 East 47th St.
New York, NY 10017–2394
212–705–7900
Serves electrical engineers with scientific, educational, and
professional activities.

International Society of Certified Electronics Technicians
2708 W. Berry St., Ste. 3
Fort Worth, TX 76109
817–921–9101
Furthers professionalism in servicing and improves the status
of electronics technicians.

National Association of Desktop Publishers
462 Old Boston St., Ste. 62
Topsfield, MA 01983
800–874–4113
Association for desktop publishing users.

National Computer Graphics Association
2722 Merrilee Dr., Ste. 200
Fairfax, VA 22031–4499
703–698–9600
Promotes computer graphics use and application development
in business, industry, science, and arts.

VGM CAREER BOOKS

CAREER DIRECTORIES
Careers Encyclopedia
Dictionary of Occupational Titles
Occupational Outlook Handbook

CAREERS FOR
Animal Lovers
Bookworms
Caring People
Computer Buffs
Crafty People
Culture Lovers
Environmental Types
Film Buffs
Foreign Language Aficionados
Good Samaritans
Gourmets
History Buffs
Kids at Heart
Nature Lovers
Night Owls
Number Crunchers
Plant Lovers
Shutterbugs
Sports Nuts
Travel Buffs
Writers

CAREERS IN
Accounting; Advertising;
Business; Child Care;
Communications; Computers;
Education; Engineering;
the Environment; Finance;
Government; Health Care; High
Tech; International Business;
Journalism; Law; Marketing;
Medicine; Science; Social &
Rehabilitation Services

CAREER PLANNING
Admissions Guide to Selective
Business Schools
Beating Job Burnout
Beginning Entrepreneur
Career Planning & Development
for College Students & Recent
Graduates
Career Change
Careers Checklists
Complete Guide to Career
Etiquette
Cover Letters They Don't Forget
Dr. Job's Complete Career Guide

Executive Job Search Strategies
Guide to Basic Cover Letter
Writing
Guide to Basic Résumé Writing
Guide to Temporary
Employment
Job Interviewing for College
Students
Joyce Lain Kennedy's Career
Book
Out of Uniform
Slam Dunk Résumés

CAREER PORTRAITS
Animals; Cars; Computers;
Electronics; Fashion;
Firefighting; Music; Nursing;
Sports; Teaching; Travel; Writing

GREAT JOBS FOR
Communications Majors
Engineering Majors
English Majors
Foreign Language Majors
History Majors
Psychology Majors

HOW TO
Approach an Advertising Agency
and Walk Away with the Job
You Want
Bounce Back Quickly After
Losing Your Job
Choose the Right Career
Cómo escribir un currículum
vitae en inglés que tenga éxito
Find Your New Career Upon
Retirement
Get & Keep Your First Job
Get Hired Today
Get into the Right Business
School
Get into the Right Law School
Get People to Do Things Your
Way
Have a Winning Job Interview
Hit the Ground Running in Your
New Job
Hold It All Together When
You've Lost Your Job
Improve Your Study Skills
Jump Start a Stalled Career
Land a Better Job

Launch Your Career in TV News
Make the Right Career Moves
Market Your College Degree
Move from College into a
Secure Job
Negotiate the Raise You Deserve
Prepare a Curriculum Vitae
Prepare for College
Run Your Own Home Business
Succeed in College
Succeed in High School
Take Charge of Your Child's
Early Education
Write a Winning Résumé
Write Successful Cover Letters
Write Term Papers & Reports
Write Your College Application
Essay

MADE EASY
Cover Letters
Job Hunting
Job Interviews
Résumés

OPPORTUNITIES IN
This extensive series provides
detailed information on nearly
150 individual career fields.

RÉSUMÉS FOR
Advertising Careers
Banking and Financial Careers
Business Management Careers
College Students &
Recent Graduates
Communications Careers
Education Careers
Engineering Careers
Environmental Careers
Ex-Military Personnel
50+ Job Hunters
Health and Medical Careers
High School Graduates
High Tech Careers
Law Careers
Midcareer Job Changes
Re-Entering the Job Market
Sales and Marketing Careers
Scientific and Technical Careers
Social Service Careers
The First-Time Job Hunter

 VGM Career Horizons
a division of *NTC Publishing Group*
4255 West Touhy Avenue
Lincolnwood, Illinois 60646–1975